Publishers: Peter L. Bannon and Joseph J. Bannon Sr.
Senior managing editor: Susan M. Moyer
Acquisitions editor: Mike Pearson
Developmental editor: Doug Hoepker
Art director: K. Jeffrey Higgerson
Dust jacket design: Dustin Hubbart
Interior layout: Kathryn R. Holleman
Photo editor: Erin Linden-Levy

Printed in the United States of America

Sports Publishing L.L.C.
804 North Neil Street
Champaign, IL 61820
Phone: 1-877-424-2665
Fax: 217-363-2073
SportsPublishingLLC.com

Library of Congress Cataloging-in-Publication Data

Monday, Rick, 1945-
Rick Monday's tales from the Dodgers dugout / Rick Monday, with Ken Gurnick ; foreword by Tommy Lasorda.
      p. cm.
ISBN 1-58261-975-1 (hardcover : alk. paper)
1. Los Angeles Dodgers (Baseball team)—History. 2. Monday, Rick, 1945-
. Title: Tales from the Dodgers dugout. II. Gurnick, Ken. III. Title.

GV875.L6.M66 2006
796.357'640979494—dc22

2006006073

Rick Monday's
Tales from the
DODGER
DUGOU

Rick Monday
with Ken Gurnick

Foreword by Tommy Lasord

SportsPublishingLLC.com

To my wife Barbaralee, who has heard these stories a few hundred times and still smiles when I retell them: Your unconditional love and support allows me to keep the memories alive. I love you.

To each and every member of the Los Angeles Dodgers "Family": I am honored to share this championship with you.

To every parent and coach who has given a youngster a reason to dream, and the courage to chase it.

To Baseball: may it forever be a game of honor and integrity.

—RM

CONTENTS

FOREWORD

BY TOMMY LASORDA

I t is only natural that Rick Monday would write a book about the Dodgers' world championship season of 1981. If not for Rick and his dramatic home run that helped us beat the Montreal Expos in the League Championship Series, we might not have been world champions that year.

But you can say the same thing for every single player who wore the Dodger uniform that season, which is one of the reasons that the fruits of victory tasted so sweet. The 1981 season—with Fernandomania and the players' strike and the remarkable three comebacks in the postseason—truly required a team effort.

Just thinking about that great season reminds me of the feeling of winning that World Series. It was the ultimate in satisfaction. We not only won the World Series, we finally defeated the New York Yankees, who had beaten us in our last two World Series appearances in 1977 and 1978.

This time, we beat them with a ball club that showed it had as much heart as talent. It was a team that consisted, in large part, of players whom I had managed since their first days as professionals. We had shared many highs and lows over the years, worked endless hours on fields at every level, and now, together, we had reached the pinnacle of our sport with the greatest comeback in baseball history, if you ask me.

It's been 25 years since our thrilling achievement, and Rick has marked the anniversary with this behind-the-scenes look back at one of the most remarkable and rewarding seasons in Dodger history. A quarter-century later, it's still an amazing story.

INTRODUCTION

BY RICK MONDAY

There has always been something magical about the Dodgers. From their revered "guts and glory" days in Brooklyn, to the "polished celebrity" of the Los Angeles club, the Dodgers have been a team with heart and soul.

Ebbets Field fans recant plays of Hall of Fame favorite Duke Snider and his teammates—Ralph Branca, Jackie Robinson, Gil Hodges, Roy Campanella, Pee Wee Reese, Don Newcombe, Carl Erskine, Clem Labine, and Preacher Roe—as though they took the field just yesterday. Los Angeles gave us the awe-inspiring excitement of Hall of Famers Sandy Koufax and Don Drysdale and the determination of Tommy Davis, Maury Wills, Lou Johnson, Willie Davis, Wes Parker, and Jim Gilliam. In the '70s, '80s, and '90s, players like Fernando Valenzuela, Orel Hershiser, Hideo Nomo, Don Sutton, Tommy John, Jimmy Wynn, Pedro Guerrero, Mike Piazza, and Steve Garvey added to an already storied past. More recently, Gary Sheffield, Paul Lo Duca, Jeff Kent, and Kevin Brown gave Angelenos a reason to come out to the park, and Eric Gagne brought the "Fever Pitch" to a new level as he welcomed us to the jungle with "GAME OVER."

Rich with history, steeped in tradition, and teeming with talent, the Los Angeles Dodgers have earned their place as a jewel in the crown of baseball. Each Dodger team—whether shining brightly, like a ruby in a gorilla's you know what, or bruised and burnished from "extra-long" seasons—has left its own footprint in the dirt of the infield. Those who came before 1981 instilled in that season's team a burning desire to "uphold the honor." I would like to believe that for those who came after us, we did the same.

It was not an easy road for us to travel in 1981. But the journey is always easier when you travel with people you can trust. In that sense, it was an easy journey. The 1981 season may have ended long ago, but the friendships have not. Each one of the gentlemen mentioned in this book has my utmost respect for what he accomplished on the field and for the professionalism displayed while doing it.

I was privileged to be their teammate; I am honored to call them friends.

DAMN YANKEES

Damn. Yankees. I'm not talking about the Ray Walston-Gwen Verdon Broadway production or its Technicolor adaptation. Certainly, there is no "Disney"-like musical accompaniment accentuating the sentiment. To the Dodgers organization, dating back to the Brooklyn days, losing to—and despising—the New York Yankees has been a way of life.

My dislike of the Yankees began prior to my arrival in Los Angeles in 1977. As best as I can remember, my dislike for the Yankees must have begun at birth. I'm not really sure why—it was just my way of life. Growing up in sunny Santa Monica, California, my life was pretty simple. Some days, my biggest decision was whether I should stop at the A&W for an orange freeze on my way to the beach or wait until I was on my way home. My days revolved around baseball, football, and surfing—in that order. And as far as baseball was concerned, I was no fan of the Yankees.

I didn't dislike anything in particular concerning the Yankees. It wasn't about their high payroll, ownership, or even locale—it was more of a general sense of disgust. The Yankees were everywhere: on

TV and radio and in print. The popular consensus was that baseball and the Yankees were synonymous. I didn't see it that way.

As a kid mesmerized by baseball, I could appreciate the play of other teams. Rooting for the underdog became my modus operandi, and I was loyal to anyone—but the Yankees. Looking back, I realize my youthful dislike wasn't limited to just the team, either. I included their players as well. It wasn't personal; it was the pinstripes.

But I made *one* exception to my rule for Mantle. "The Mick." Mickey Mantle was *the man*. While the rest of my schoolmates would rant and rave about the Yankees, I'd silently burn until Mantle's name came up. He could run, he could field, he could hit with power. He could leap tall buildings in a single bound! There was just something "magical" about Mantle. As a player he was larger than life and the one redeeming quality of the Yankees. To me, he was not a Yankee—he was baseball.

But as for the rest of the Yankees, I could have cared less. Fast forward 20 years and I realized my instincts were right. I hated them for good reason. Only now it wasn't the pinstripes. Now it was personal.

GONE HOLLYWOOD

As a Dodger, I lost to the Yankees in the 1977 World Series, highlighted by Reggie Jackson hitting three home runs in one game. The frustration of losing after coming so far only added to my dislike of that team. After all we had accomplished to get to the World Series and, as usual, what people remember are the Yankees.

In my opinion, that 1977 Dodgers team was the best one that I ever played for. That was my first year with the Dodgers, after the Chicago Cubs traded me to Los Angeles for Bill Buckner. I found myself in a rather new, unfamiliar, and yet exciting situation. Where the Cubbies were everybody's "sentimental favorite," the Dodgers were a part of Hollywood royalty. When celebrities wanted a night off, they would come to the ballpark and watch us; when we wanted a night off, we went to the movie theater to watch them.

For "Hollywood Stars Night" at the ballpark, one could see the likes of Annette Funicello, Danny Kaye, Dyan Cannon, The Captain and Tennille, Tony Orlando, Jonathan Winters, Don Rickles, and a marquee list of others. Winters would occasionally drop by the clubhouse and do an impromptu stand-up baseball routine. Dodger Stadium was dotted with big-time celebrities like Frank Sinatra, Dean Martin, Walter Matthau, Jack Lemmon, and other A-list Hollywood heavyweights just about every night. The national anthem was a notable venue of its own, sung by chart-topping musicians. As I recall, early in that season, Sinatra was one such notable performer. I was experiencing a celebrity of sorts myself, having gained some national notoriety after rescuing the American flag from two would-be flag burners at Dodger Stadium the previous season while playing centerfield with the Chicago Cubs.

What was unique is that 1977 was actually a "new season" for the entire team. Tommy Lasorda took over the helm from eventual Hall of Fame manager Walt Alston, who skippered the team for 23 years. Little did we know at the time, but Tommy was embarking on a Hall of Fame managerial career of his own.

In Dodger lore, 1977 should go down as a remarkable season for a talented team. We showed, from the very first day of spring training, that we did not want to lose—not even an exhibition game. As teammates, we made it our business to challenge ourselves to play to our full potential. Among fan favorites at that time were Ron Cey, Bill Russell, Davey Lopes, and Steve Garvey, who began playing as a unit in 1973 and would spend a record eight and a half seasons together. In '77, the Dodgers made history when four members of the team hit 30 or more home runs: Garvey (33), Reggie Smith (32), Cey (30), and Dusty Baker (30).

The season itself was also one of the Dodgers' most notable. Five of our starters—Tommy John, Don Sutton, Doug Rau, Burt Hooton, and Rick Rhoden—won at least 12 games, with John winning 20 and our ace and Opening Day starter, Sutton, being named the All-Star Game MVP. Steve Garvey was the focal point of the offense. The top vote-getter in fan balloting, Garvey homered in the National League's 7-5 All-Star Game win. We clinched the division title against the archrival San Francisco Giants, and Dusty Baker carried us to victory over the Phillies in the National League Championship Series and into the World Series, where Reggie Jackson put on his show.

"We thought we should have won in '77," says Garvey of the team's trip to the World Series. "It was the best team I ever played on. And you figure, if you're lucky as a professional, you get to the World Series once, probably not twice and certainly not three times. So considering what happened in '81, it makes you wonder if we weren't destined to win a world championship."

A FAMILY BUSINESS

Ownership was a driving force of that '77 team. Chemistry was a key ingredient for that team, and ownership set the tone, leading by example. The importance of the Walter O'Malley legacy should not be taken lightly; if you were a player, you wanted to play for O'Malley's Dodgers.

From the beginning of time, history repeatedly proves that a strong foundation is the key to longevity, and the O'Malleys were no stranger to this concept. An organization unique for its family values and atmosphere, starting with Walter O'Malley, the Dodgers operation grew to be the envy of baseball. Christmas at Dodgertown, St. Patrick's Day, Old Timer's Day, the Dodger Family Game, wives flying any time, anywhere, with their husbands on the team plane. It was not an organization. It truly was a family.

"The St. Patrick's Day Party was the first spring training function, even though the players weren't involved. That started back in the barracks days in the early Fifties," recalls Peter O'Malley, Walter's son and the leader of the team ownership group from 1970 through 1998. "The Christmas Party was (former Dodgertown director) Charlie

The O'Malleys—Peter (left) and his father, Walter—at Dodgertown during spring training. Peter kept the Dodgers "in the family" once his father passed away in 1979, while also maintaining the family atmosphere that had become a trademark of the organization.

Blaney's idea. We were never together in December, and with all of the kids around during spring training, he thought it would be a good idea to put it together, and it worked.

"I think our best function was the Easter Egg Hunt. Coy Hunter, the wife of one of our writers, Bob Hunter, was the Easter Bunny. All of these events just brought people together. The staff, the players, even the media. It worked great."

Mike Scioscia agrees: "I didn't realize at the time, but the years have put in perspective what the support from the top down means. At the time, you think every organization is just like yours. Now, 30 years later, you understand what a special dynamic was at work with the Dodger organization then.

"Starting with Peter O'Malley and his sister, Terry Seidler, down to Al Campanis and Walter Alston and Tommy Lasorda and Fred Claire. With Peter and Terry, it had to be the best ownership in any professional sport. We were very fortunate the way they embraced everyone as family."

I was 17 the first time I met Walter O'Malley. Fresh out of Santa Monica High, I had earned a spot on the Dodger-sponsored "Dodger Rookies," a recruit-rich team of recently graduated seniors and the occasional college freshman, which the Dodgers had interest in signing. Tommy Lasorda, then a Dodger scout, wanted to sign me to a professional contract, so he invited my mother and me to visit Dodger Stadium to watch a game. After touring the facilities, we stopped by the O'Malley family suite for an introduction. Even now, I recall two things about that moment. One, the absolute awe I felt in meeting Walter O'Malley, the "larger-than-life" owner of the Los Angeles Dodgers. And two, the gracious and respectful manner in which he addressed my mom.

Having been left on our own years earlier, my life revolved around my mom. She worked, struggled, and sacrificed so that I could pursue "the dream." I loved, honored, adored, and respected her—and everyone else had better do the same. Both warm and courteous, O'Malley visited with my mom as though he had known her for years.

In his presence, you had a sense of the familiar as you do with your family. Warm and reassuring, he told my mom that the Dodgers "would take good care of Rick. We have the best coaches, the best facilities in baseball, and it would be great for him to be able to play right here at home." And then I heard the words that were music to my ears: "Mrs. Monday, we are really interested in having Rick sign with the Dodgers. With everything Tommy has told us, he really has a chance to play here at Dodger Stadium." Inside the Stadium, standing there in front of O'Malley, I felt at home.

At the time, however, a few colleges were also recruiting me. I had spoken with San Fernando Valley State (now California State Northridge) about going there. Their freshman assistant coach was a guy named Dick Enberg, who went into another line of work as a successful sports broadcaster. I spoke with Cal Poly Pomona a few times and Southern California and Rod Dedeaux just about every week for two months.

Coach Bobby Winkles came over from Arizona State University to watch me play a game for the "Dodger Rookies." During the game my mom sat with Bobby and he told her about his program. After the game, Winkles offered me a scholarship. Bobby and my mom had obviously hit it off real well. The decision to attend ASU and play for Bobby was one of the greatest decisions I've ever made. The respect I have for that man is unwavering.

My decision to attend ASU in no way discounted Tommy Lasorda's or the Dodgers' attempts to sign me. In fact, Tommy took my mother and me out for dinner one night and he presented a contract to my mom for me to sign with the Dodgers. My mother actually had a pen in her hand three different times to sign the contract, only to put the pen down and tell Tommy that she wanted me to go to college first, after which I would sign with the Dodgers.

Every time she did that, Tommy took back the contract, scribbled out the dollar amount, and increased it substantially, only to have my mom put the pen down again. She wasn't trying to negotiate. She just felt very strongly that, with me being only 17 years old, I needed to go to college. So I did. None of us knew then that the "free agent draft" was just around the corner. I wound up as the first player taken in baseball's initial draft in 1965, joining the Kansas City Athletics.

But I never stopped wanting to be a Dodger, which is why that visit with Walter O'Malley meant so much to me.

Wonderfully, once I joined the Dodgers, it was clear they were everything I had envisioned. The O'Malleys worked hard to make the organization a family. One never heard "Dodger organization." It was "Dodger family." I think for all of us, this was pivotal to the success of those ball clubs. The old cliché, "There is no 'I' in team," held true for everyone. Ownership, front office, players, and personnel alike—we worked together, lost together, played together, and won together. Truth be known, we laughed together and cried together, too. The O'Malleys looked after us and cared for us all—and together we would eat, sleep, and drink baseball. We didn't know it then, but those were "the glory days."

Years later, you will hear players, from Brooklyn on down, admirably and with great love, speak of the O'Malley family. I think for all of us, the Dodgers were our family, and families are forever.

HIP CHECKS AREN'T JUST FOR HOCKEY

The 1978 World Series brought yet another loss to the Yankees, and our team's dislike for the boys from the Bronx grew with fervor. In the sixth inning of a crucial Game 4, with the Dodgers leading 3-0 in the game and 2-1 in the series, Reggie Jackson singled home a run to cut into our lead. Lou Piniella followed Jackson by bouncing a tailor-made double-play ball to shortstop Bill Russell. The inning appeared to be over. Russell stepped on second then flipped toward first. Jackson was midway between first and second—too far from second to disrupt Russell with a slide. So Jackson stopped running, shifted his hip into the path of Russell's throw, and caused the ball to carom into right field as a run scored. Jackson got away with a flagrant and intentional violation of the rule book, something to which Jackson would admit in the years to follow, thus bringing yet another world championship chance to a bitter end. Jackson's play ended up a deciding factor in a game we lost—and left us feeling cheated.

In retrospect, I grudgingly admit that the Yankees were a team to be reckoned with and respected. As a franchise, they "came to play," and in turn, made you play as well. Playing against them was, oftentimes, like watching baseball at its best. You didn't like to play the Yankees because they had so many players who could beat you. Thurman Munson led the team from behind the plate, and Graig Nettles was an octopus at third. As if he wore eight different gloves, he'd scoop everything hit anywhere near him. Piniella's bat was a force to be reckoned with, and Jackson was just building upon his reputation as "Mr. October." Offensively and defensively, Mickey Rivers, Chris Chambliss, and Bucky Dent could hurt you in ways you never dreamed of. And then there was the pitching staff: Catfish Hunter, Ron Guidry, Rich Gossage, and Sparky Lyle could light up your night.

It was obvious to all that the Dodgers were a force on the rise and the Yankees were our Achilles' heel. We had a team much like the previous year, led by Sutton, who made his seventh Opening Day start, Hooton, who won 19 games, and the awesome hitting of Garvey and Smith. Our fans again showed they were the best in baseball, this time surpassing the three-million mark in attendance at Dodger Stadium, the first time in Major League history such a feat had occurred. We clinched the division during the season's final weekend, won a thrilling National League Championship Series against the Phillies, only to suffer the letdown of losing to the Yankees again in the World Series.

We did, however, witness a classic confrontation between pitcher and hitter in that World Series: Bob Welch against Reggie Jackson, power pitcher versus power hitter. The rookie Welch, trying to protect a one-run lead in the ninth inning with two runners on, worked Jackson to a 3-2 count. Welch fired three straight fastballs and Jackson fouled off each one, but took a mighty swing and a miss on the fourth and struck out to end the game. It captured the truest essence and emotion of the World Series.

As champions in our own right, that '78 Dodger team was an equal contender. A proud franchise, we had certainly earned bragging rights. But we hadn't done enough to be true champions, and time was running out.

WHEN'S OUR TURN?

By the time the 1981 season rolled around, the nucleus of those Dodger teams had pretty much run its course. The clock was ticking. But there was unfinished business. We desperately wanted another chance to win a world championship. And we especially wanted another chance to beat the Yankees in the World Series.

When I set out to share the inside story of the 1981 Dodger season, I was curious to know if other former teammates recalled the same images that have been etched in my mind and heart (not to mention my aching bones) for all these years. Did they remember the competitive edge that had burned inside their bellies so many years ago? Was the memory of all that hard work, sacrifice, and togetherness still fresh for them? If I still knew these gentlemen like I did so many years ago, then nothing would have faded from their memories. To a man, each of them embodied a commitment to winning, and a respect for one another and the game of baseball! And they proved it every day on the baseball field. They hated to lose. And even more so, they *hated to lose to the Yankees.*

Reflecting on the past brings to mind events of the present. The season itself, fantasy camps, conventions, signings and the like, offer me, and most of my teammates, the opportunity to reconnect and reminisce. We're now diversified individuals sifting through the memories of a common denominator. One of my teammates, Dusty Baker, has gone on to a managerial career as accomplished as his playing-day career. It was reassuring to hear from Dusty that I wasn't the only one who still felt that the losses in 1977 and 1978 were an underlying motivator for the unforgettable season we had in 1981.

"Quite honestly, I was tired of seeing the Yankees," remembers Baker. "As a kid growing up a Dodgers fan in Southern California, they used to beat the Dodgers all the time. And then, when I got to the big leagues with the Dodgers, they beat us all the time.

"In '78, that was probably the worst one, because we had gone up two games to nothing. I remember, we were playing for Jim Gilliam [the Dodger coach who died two days before the series opened], we had "Devil's" No. 19 on our sleeve, and man, we were up 2-0 and they beat us three in a row at Yankee Stadium—we just couldn't believe it. Then we went back home, for one game, and they beat us again."

You could pretty much go up and down the list of Dodgers who had lost to the Yankees in 1977 and 1978 and were still on the club in 1981, and they would have told you the same thing: there was a score to settle.

"I just had this great big payback for '77 and '78 that I wanted to take care of," recalls Ron Cey. "Not just '77, but '78 in particular, because that's my most disappointing moment in all of baseball, to lose that World Series under those circumstances and have the Reggie Jackson incident, when the entire series might have come to a different point if [umpire] Frank Pulli would've just said: 'You know what, I think I better huddle with these other guys [like they do today] and make sure we get this thing right.' We'd have been walking off the field into the seventh inning with a 3-1 lead."

Pulli rejected manager Tommy Lasorda's protests of interference, and the Yankees came back to win the game in 10 innings, 4-3, shifting momentum in the series. Just makes you sick, doesn't it? It still does to me, too.

But before we get too far into what happened in 1981, let's run down the list of players who made it happen. Every player on the 1981 team understood he had a role to play and knew what it took to prepare for each game. No one player or group of players was more important than the other, whether you were a starting position player, pitcher, or backup player. We were a team, a complete package, with an inner toughness I don't believe I ever experienced on any other team. We knew how to play the game. Four of us—Russell, Lopes, Baker, and Scioscia—went on to manage in the Major Leagues. We loved challenges, and if you were going to beat us, then you had to beat all of us. Besides sharing World Series championship rings, I believe each and every one of us will always share a great respect for one another.

2

THE NAMES AND THE FACES

A s I've said on numerous occasions already, the Dodgers were like a big family. So this chapter is dedicated to introducing the cast of characters in my family in 1981, in alphabetical order.

DR. SCALD

Dusty Baker wasn't selected until the 25th round of the 1967 amateur draft, but don't let that fool you: he was a natural talent. He batted .342 at Greenwood to earn a call-up to the Braves in September 1968 at age 19. By age 26, he had four productive Major League seasons under his belt. The Dodgers paid a steep price to get Baker from the Braves after the 1975 season, acquiring him and infielder Ed Goodson for Jimmy Wynn, Tom Paciorek, Jerry Royster, and Lee Lacy.

While he was with the Braves, Dusty Baker learned lessons from Hank Aaron that helped him emerge as a feared offensive force in 1981.

From the beginning, though, it was a perfect fit. Baker, a Riverside, California, native grew up a Dodger fan idolizing Tommy Davis, and so he wore Davis's No. 12 while with the Dodgers. He predominantly played left field and was a consistent contributor during his eight years in Los Angeles. He played 149 or more games in six of those seasons, often with a flair for the dramatic. On September 5, 1981, Baker was sidelined with a heavy cold, but entered a game against the Cardinals in the 11th inning and clubbed a pinch-hit, walk-off homer off Jim Kaat.

Baker had one of his best power seasons in 1980, batting .294 with 29 homers and 97 RBI en route to winning a Silver Slugger Award. But his 1981 season was arguably his finest all-around effort, as Baker hit a career-high .320, made his first All-Star team, won his only Gold Glove, and again took home the Silver Slugger. Only Bill Madlock and Pete Rose finished with a better average at the plate.

Baker was also a major contributor in the National League Championship Series that season, batting .316 against the Expos. But Baker broke his hand in a parking lot fight with a pair of Expos fans and spent the World Series playing through pain, serving as a decoy in the lineup against the Yankees, who were unaware of Baker's injury. He batted .167 while playing in all six games.

"Dr. Scald" was one of his nicknames on the club as he could really scald a fastball. One of the funniest lines I remember from Dusty came during a game one night at Dodger Stadium after he was retired by an opposing pitcher. The pitcher had laughed out loud after getting Baker out. Dusty came back to the dugout fuming and finally turned and yelled out to the pitcher, "Go ahead and laugh, the next time I'm going to hit you so hard, it'll knock the spit right out of your mouth!" Sure enough, that's just what he did.

Baker played two more seasons with the Dodgers and retired after 1986 at the age of 37 with a very respectable career hit total: 1,981. After his playing career ended, he remained in baseball as a coach and took over as the manager in San Francisco in 1993. He promptly led the Giants to 103 wins that year, but that was only good enough for a second-place finish in the NL West. He managed 10 seasons in San Francisco, finishing second or first in eight of them and compiling a .540 winning percentage. In 2002, he managed the Giants to the World Series, but the team fell to the Angels in seven games.

The following season Baker moved on to Chicago, where he currently manages the Cubs and is still searching for a managerial championship to match the one he earned as a player with the Dodgers. It is no surprise to those of us who were his teammates to see him go on to be a successful manager. He knows what makes people tick.

WHAT A SCREWBALL

Bobby Castillo, or "Babo" as we called him, had a great sense of humor and a terrific screwball. He had a certain intensity on the mound, possessing a "street fighter"-like mentality. A Los Angeles native, Castillo led the Dodger bullpen in innings pitched in 1980, posting a 2.75 ERA. He had a difficult 1981, including a one-inning appearance in the Dodgers' 5-3 loss in the World Series opener in which he walked five batters.

Castillo did get off to a strong start that year, however, as a key member of our bullpen, posting a 3.86 ERA in seven April appearances while saving three games. But with the strength of the Dodger pitching staff that season, Castillo had a hard time getting consistent work as the season progressed, and he failed to post a sub-4.00 ERA in any other month that year. Perhaps the most outstanding part of Castillo's 1981 campaign came at the plate, where he was 4-for-9 with two doubles.

His greatest achievement, of course, was being credited with teaching fellow Mexican Fernando Valenzuela the screwball during the Arizona Instructional League. We all know how that worked out for Valenzuela in 1981.

Bobby Castillo emerged as an important part of the bullpen during the Dodgers' torrid start to the 1981 season.

Castillo was traded to Minnesota after the season. Given a chance to start in 1982, the righthander put together a career-best season, going 13-11 with a 3.66 ERA in 218⅓ innings. After two more years with the Twins, Castillo returned to finish his career with the Dodgers in 1985. He made one start in the 1985 NLCS, allowing only two runs in 5⅓ innings but picking up a no-decision in the Dodgers' Game 4 loss.

Today, Castillo remains an active member of the Los Angeles community, working in the Dodgers' Speakers Bureau.

THE PENGUIN

Ron Cey was nicknamed "Penguin" because, well, he moves like one, with a sort of waddle. He had a quiet, no-nonsense approach that was fortified with an inner toughness you had to be around every day to fully appreciate. We saw that toughness toward the end of the 1981 season as he dealt with two different injuries that appeared to be catastrophic. But with Ron, if there wasn't a bone showing, he was going to play.

He was a grumpy Penguin when his productive 1981 campaign was cut short by a Tom Griffin fastball that fractured his left forearm September 9, forcing him to the sidelines for the rest of the regular season. Little more than a month later, though, Cey returned to action at third base in the playoffs, hitting .278 in the NLCS and .350 with six RBI in the World Series. He was hit in the head by a Goose Gossage fastball in Game 5, but shook off a concussion to play in Game 6. A symbol of perseverance and courage, as well as production, he was named one of the Dodgers' World Series MVPs and was also honored with the NL Babe Ruth Award.

During the 1981 season, Cey hit eight homers in a 15-game stretch, tallied 10 hits in 13 at-bats, had a five-hit game, a four-hit game, and six three-hit games and led the club with nine game-winning RBI. Cey's .288 average that year was the best of his career, but due to the strike and the fractured arm, he hit only 13 home

Ron Cey played with a lot of heart and, as he showed during the 1981 season, through a lot of pain, too.

runs—the only year from 1976 to 1985 that he didn't slug at least 22 round-trippers.

The Tacoma native belted his 200th career homer May 23, 1981, and finished with 316 Major League home runs. After playing 12 years in Los Angeles, Cey played four seasons with the Cubs before closing out his career with Oakland in 1987. The best years of Cey's career came with the Dodgers, who selected him in the third round of Al Campanis's legendary 1968 draft. (In that draft, the Dodgers also selected Bobby Valentine, Steve Garvey, Doyle Alexander, and Bill Buckner.) Cey rewarded the Dodgers with six consecutive All-Star seasons from 1974 to 1979. A patient hitter who often ranked among the league leaders in walks, hit-by-pitches, and sacrifice flies, Cey finished with 842 RBI in 1,480 games as a Dodger.

Lesser known amongst his Dodger "records" is the album he cut in 1976 that featured classic tunes like "Playin' the Third Base Bag" and "One Game at a Time." His recording career never took off like his baseball career, however. Today, Cey is back with the Dodgers, working in their marketing department.

"A FAT TUB OF GOO"

Lefthander Terry Forster was the first free agent the Dodgers had ever signed. He joined the Blue Crew in 1978 and didn't disappoint, going 5-4 with a 1.93 ERA and 22 saves. From there, though, things went downhill. Forster underwent elbow surgeries in 1978 and 1979 to remove bone spurs and relocate an irritated nerve. He continued his comeback from elbow surgery in 1981. Although he pitched only 21 times, he nonetheless logged more innings during the strike-shortened season than he was able to pitch in the two previous seasons combined. Forster was so hyper he could make a cup of coffee nervous. Even though he constantly pitched with a painful elbow, he always had a smile or a laugh to offer his teammates.

Serving as the Dodgers' second left-hander in the bullpen behind Steve Howe, Forster was particularly effective in September (1.32 ERA in nine games) and in the postseason, when he allowed only one hit in four appearances. After his strong finish to the 1981 season, though, Forster was able to pitch 224 games over the next five seasons with the Dodgers, Braves, and Angels. He finished his 16-year career with a 3.23 ERA and 127 saves. However, the San Diego native probably received more attention for being called "a fat tub of goo" by late-night comedian David Letterman than for anything he did on the field. Today, Forster lives thousands of miles from Southern California, in Val D'or, Quebec.

GARV

Steve Garvey was the son of a bus driver who often chauffeured the Dodgers to and from their spring complex in Florida. As a youngster, he served as a spring-training batboy for the club. He graduated from Michigan State in 1971 with a B.S. in education, having earned All-America honors in baseball in addition to starting on the Spartans' football team as a defensive back.

He was drafted by the Dodgers with the 13th overall pick in that remarkable 1968 draft and made his big-league debut one year later. But throwing problems for the then-third baseman necessitated a shift to first base, and he didn't win an everyday job until 1974, when he tallied 200 hits for the first of six times in his career and won the NL MVP award by hitting 21 homers and driving in 111 runs. That year, he made the All-Star Game as a write-in candidate and won the Midsummer Classic's MVP award, going 2-for-4 with an RBI double. He also picked up his first of four consecutive Gold Glove awards that season.

By the late '70s, Garvey had become a near-lock for a .300 average and 100 RBI. But he did not have one of his best seasons in 1981— until it counted the most, batting .359 in the playoffs and .417 in the World Series. During the regular season, Garvey tallied nine three-hit games and drove in five runs in a game against the Pirates. He led the Dodger charge in May, when he hit .329 and drove in 22 runs.

When you arrived in the locker room every day, the starting lineup was posted on the board. Unless "Garv" had been scooped up by an alien he would be in the lineup, just like the rest of the record-breaking Dodger infielders. Garvey played in every one of the Dodgers' games in 1981 for the sixth consecutive year, giving him 945 consecutive games played en route to his league record of 1,207 games in a row. While his .283 average was his lowest mark in a decade, Garvey nonetheless ranked in the NL top 10 in hits, doubles, runs, and RBI. He also led NL first basemen in fielding percentage (.999), committing only one error in 1,075 chances.

After 14 years as a Los Angeles fixture, Garvey joined the Padres as a free agent in 1983. The right-handed hitter had his best days with the Dodgers, though, as he never drove in more than 86 runs for the Padres, for whom he batted .275 over the course of five seasons. He did, however, win the NLCS MVP award for his play in the 1984 playoffs.

Garvey retired at 38, having tallied 2,559 hits and 1,308 RBI in his career. He set marks for consecutive NL games played and consecutive errorless games at first base (193). The ten-time All-Star hit .300 or better in eight of his 11 career postseason series, smacking 11 home runs and driving in 31 runs in 55 playoff games.

Today, the fan favorite makes Palm Desert, California, his home, and works in the Dodgers' marketing department.

HE'S NO SINKERBALLER

Dave Goltz, who won 20 games for the Twins in 1977, came to the Dodgers with the label "sinkerball" pitcher. Supposedly, Dodgers general manager Al Campanis never saw him pitch prior to his arrival in Los Angeles, and signed the free agent off the strength of scouting reports. Those reports proved to be wrong: Dave, it turned out, was not a "sinkerball" pitcher. He struggled in his first season with Los

Angeles in 1980, going 7-11 with a 4.32 ERA. But no one tried harder than Goltz, and despite a demotion to the long-relief role of the pen, he improved somewhat in 1981.

In the 1981 playoffs, Goltz didn't pitch until the World Series, when he made two appearances. In Game 4, Bob Welch was pulled after allowing three hits and a walk without retiring a batter. Goltz came in and threw three innings, allowing two runs, in the Dodgers' eventual 8-7 victory.

After being released by the Dodgers early in the 1982 season, Goltz signed with the Angles and went a respectable 8-5 with a 4.08 ERA. He retired after going 0-6 with a 6.22 ERA for the Angels in 1983. Despite the rough finish, Goltz's career record was a winning one: 113-109, with a 3.69 ERA.

Goltz now resides in his native state of Minnesota, where he enjoys hunting and fishing.

YOUNG SLUGGER ARRIVES

The first thing you noticed about Pedro Guerrero was his bat speed. His swing was almost flawless. Trying to get a fastball past him was impossible. That swing made him arguably the finest Dodger hitter of the 1980s.

Guerrero came to Los Angeles cheaply: He was acquired from Cleveland in 1974 in exchange for pitcher Bruce Ellingsen, who played his first and last season in the Majors that year. But Guerrero wouldn't stick with the Dodgers until 1980, at which time he was out of options. He ended the year hitting .322 in limited playing time.

The following year, he established himself as one of the best bats in the Dodger lineup. In 1981, Guerrero contributed a .300 average, 31 extra-base hits and 48 RBI while playing regularly in right field before shifting to third base after Cey went on the disabled list. He finished eighth in the NL with a .464 slugging percentage. Despite his fine regular season, "Pete" undoubtedly saved his best for last. In Game 6 of the World Series, his three-hit, five-RBI game propelled us

Pedro Guerrero used the 1981 season to show the rest of baseball why the Dodgers had been so high on him.

to a 9-2 clinching victory and earned the 25-year-old a share of Series MVP honors. After struggling in the first two rounds of the playoffs, he finished the Fall Classic 7-for-21 with two homers and seven RBI.

Guerrero's World Series heroics foreshadowed a tremendous career as a power hitter. He hit 32 homers with 100-plus RBI in 1982 and 1983, and in 1987 he batted a career-best .338 with 27 round-trippers. He was only the 12th Dodger in franchise history to reach the 30-homer plateau. His finest all-around season came in 1985, when he batted .320, drew a career-high 83 walks and slugged 22 doubles and 33 homers. Not only did Guerrero lead the league in on-base percentage (.422), he also ranked first in slugging (.577). He finished third that year in MVP voting for the second time in his career.

During the 1988 season, Guerrero was traded to the St. Louis Cardinals for John Tudor, and retired five years later at the age of 36 with a career batting average of .300.

HARDLY "HAPPY"

Nicknamed "Happy" because he never looked it, Burt Hooton came equipped with a knuckle-curveball, a dry sense of humor, and flawless timing. Dodger Hall of Fame broadcaster Vin Scully summed up Burt the best by saying that "Happy" celebrated the world championship by going out and "painting the town beige."

Acquired from the Cubs in 1975 for two reliable but unexceptional starters—Geoff Zahn and Eddie Solomon—Hooton posted a sub-3.00 ERA in five of his first seven seasons in Los Angeles. He was a career-best119-10 in 1978 with a 2.71 ERA and finished his Dodger career 112-84.

The crafty righthander had one of his better seasons for the Dodgers in 1981, bouncing back from shoulder bursitis to go 11-6 with a career-best 2.28 ERA. He won his first seven decisions in 1981 and closed the season with equal effectiveness, allowing only two earned runs in his final 21 innings. He allowed only three home runs in 142⅓ innings and ranked third in the league with four shutouts.

More importantly, he was our best pitcher in postseason play, going 4-1 with a 0.82 ERA in five starts in 1981. In the NLCS against Montreal, he won Games 1 and 4, allowing only one unearned run in 14⅔ innings to be named series MVP. He also led our turnaround in the Division Series, earning the Dodgers' first victory of the series in Game 3 by allowing three hits and one run in seven innings. After suffering a tough loss in Game 2 of the World Series, Hooton won the series clincher, allowing two runs in 5⅓ innings.

Happy left the Dodgers for the Texas Rangers as a free agent prior to his final season in the Majors in 1985. He finished with a 3.38 ERA and 151 wins. He made his only All-Star team in 1981. After his playing career ended, Hooton went on to serve as a pitching coach with the Astros organization and now lives in Houston.

A TROUBLED LEFTY

Steve Howe, the 1980 NL Rookie of the Year, picked up where he left off in 1981, improving his ERA and recording a team-high eight saves. The postseason was equally kind to Howe, who posted a 2.45 ERA in seven games. In Game 4 of the World Series, he earned the win by throwing three innings of relief. And in the clincher, he relieved Hooton in the sixth inning and threw 3⅔ innings of two-hit relief to earn the save. Imagine a closer pitching that many innings in a game today!

As the Dodgers' first-round selection in the 1979 draft, Howe had to live up to plenty of hype. He became the winningest pitcher in University of Michigan history in only three seasons, going 27-8 with a 1.79 ERA. He threw a one-hit shutout in the opener of the 1978 College World Series and earned All-America honors in 1979. For a time, Howe fulfilled the immense expectations. By his third season in 1982, he was an All-Star putting up dominant numbers (2.08 ERA).

At a young age and with little experience, a brash Steve Howe became the most dominant left-handed reliever in the National League.

His success continued in 1983 as he saved a career-best 18 games and posted a miniscule 1.44 ERA.

But then an addiction to cocaine stalled his baseball career. Howe battled his addiction throughout his career, and it kept him off the field for five full seasons as well as parts of others. Commissioner Bowie Kuhn suspended Howe for one full season in December 1983, after the reliever tested positive for cocaine on three occasions and pleaded guilty to federal charges of attempting to possess cocaine. Even after returning to the field in 1985, though, Howe continued to relapse, and the Dodgers released him in July of that year.

The following month, he signed with the Twins, but fared no better there. Between the end of the 1985 season and the start of the 1991 season, Howe appeared in only 24 games (for Texas in 1997). He joined the Yankees in 1991 and spent parts of six seasons in the Bronx, although he continued to struggle with drug use, being suspended multiple times and being convicted for trying to purchase cocaine in Montana in 1992 and for having a loaded gun in his suitcase at JFK Airport in 1996, his final year in the Majors.

Despite all the distractions, Howe was one of the best lefthanded relievers in the game. In two of his first four seasons with the Yankees he posted an ERA under 2.00, including a 15-save season in 1994. Howe finished his career 47-41 with 91 saves and a 3.03 ERA.

Let us not allow the future to overshadow the past. Howe became as dominant as anyone out of the bullpen. Always liked by his teammates, he had a quick sense of humor, and we have always wanted the best for him.

"HOT-FOOT" ARTIST

If you had a two-minute conversation on the bench with "Jaybird," as we called Jay Johnstone, and didn't get a "hot foot," your day was a success. Johnstone was famous for lighting his teammates' shoelaces on fire. Beyond all the funny stuff Jay would do before,

All you need to know about Jay Johnstone is that he wrote a book about his playing days and titled it *Temporary Insanity*. It wasn't temporary—and he fit right in.

during, and after games, he has always had a terrific passion for baseball.

He didn't play much in 1981, but he certainly made it count when he did. The outfielder was 11-for-38 (.289) with three homers as a pinch-hitter and had a knack for coming through in the most important situations. His pinch-hit, two-run homer in Game 4 of the World Series was the catalyst for our comeback in that game and the series as a whole. He finished the Fall Classic 2-for-3 with three RBI. Postseason success was Johnstone's forte: He was 7-for-9 in the 1976 NLCS with Philadelphia.

Released by the Dodgers in May 1982, he was quickly claimed by the Cubs, where he played for three seasons before finishing his career with the Dodgers in 1985. In 20 Major League seasons, Johnstone batted .267 with 102 homers.

One of the 1981 squad's most entertaining players, Johnstone was a member of the "Big Blue Wrecking Crew" recording group, along with Jerry Reuss, Steve Yeager, and me. The Southern California native authored three baseball books, owned an automotive business in Los Angeles while with the Dodgers, and currently resides in Pasadena.

LATE ADDITION

Ken Landreaux, acquired for Mickey Hatcher at the end of the 1981 spring training, was a fixture in the Dodgers outfield for the rest of his career. He didn't have a strong offensive year in 1981, but his speed and defense in center field helped us just the same. He stole 18 bases in only 22 attempts and did not commit an error all season. Fittingly, it was Landreaux who secured Bob Watson's fly ball for the final out of the World Series.

The lefthanded hitter had a much better first half of the season (.270 before the strike vs. .229 after), but had a few highlights in the second half, including his first multi-homer game on August 19 in Chicago. "K.T." was a graceful player both in the outfield and at home plate. He had a quick bat, and many pitchers were surprised when he turned on one of their hard pitches inside.

A Los Angeles native, Landreaux attended Dominguez Hills High School and was the Angels' first-round pick in the 1976 draft. He spent time in the majors the following season and soon found his name in baseball record books. In his first Major League game, he threw out three base runners, and in 1980 he put together a 31-game hitting streak, setting a Twins club record. Also in 1980, he tied a Major League record by hitting three triples in a game, after tying another record in 1979 by doubling twice in the same inning.

Landreaux spent the final seven seasons of his career with the Dodgers. He hit better than .280 with more than 30 steals in both 1982 and 1983. Landreaux concluded his career with 1,099 career hits and today works in the Dodgers' Speakers Bureau.

THE SKIPPER AT HIS BEST

Some people may not agree with me on this subject, but I think Tommy Lasorda had his best year yet as manager in 1981. Oh, he had a great start to begin the season. But then with all he had to deal with—the strike, a declared first-half and second-half winner, extra playoff formats, and just holding a ball club together—1981 was Tommy at his best.

SPEED PLUS POWER

One of the best base runners in Major League history, second baseman Davey Lopes was drafted by the Dodgers in 1968 and spent the first 10 years of his career in Dodger Blue. He played sparingly in 1981, hampered by lingering back, hamstring, and neck injuries, and spent time on the disabled list with a groin injury. Despite the ailments, though, Lopes was a terror on the base paths in the 1981 postseason, stealing 10 bases in 10 attempts.

Davey Lopes had a bittersweet season in 1981. He finally won a world championship, but was plagued during the year by injuries that hastened his trade to Oakland after the season.

Lopes scored six of the Dodgers' runs in the World Series, reaching base nine times and stealing four bases. It proved a fitting end to his Dodger career, as the second baseman was traded to the A's following the 1981 season for Lance Hudson, an outfielder who never made the Majors. By trading Lopes, Los Angeles broke up the longest-running infield in Major League history, as Cey, Garvey, Lopes, and shortstop Bill Russell had played together for 8½ seasons.

Years ago, Maury Wills changed the thinking in baseball in regard to what speed can do for a baseball team. Today we know that speed can disrupt the pitcher and force defensive mistakes. Lopes's speed was put to good use at the top of the batting order—but he added the dimension of power in the leadoff position. Davey was our table setter, but pitchers had to respect him as a hitter as well as a runner. In 1979, he hit a team-best 28 homers out of the lead-off spot.

Lopes had innumerable highlights with the Dodgers, including winning a Gold Glove, a then-record 38 consecutive steals without being caught in 1975, four consecutive All-Star appearances (including 1981), back-to-back stolen base titles in the mid-'70s, and five homers and 12 RBI in the 1978 postseason. After leaving the Dodgers, Lopes continued to enjoy success with the A's, Cubs, and Astros. He stole 47 bases in 51 attempts at the age of 40 while batting a career-best .284 for the Cubs. Lopes finished his career with a .263 average, 155 homers, and 557 steals in 671 attempts for an astounding 83 percent success rate, which currently ranks among the 10 best career marks in history.

During Lopes's career, players such as Tom Seaver and Johnny Bench compared him to speed demon Lou Brock, while Maury Wills called Lopes "the greatest base stealer in the game today."

Lopes graduated from Iowa Wesleyan College and taught elementary education. After his playing career ended, he put those teaching skills to use, coaching for the University of Texas before managing Milwaukee from 2000 to 2002. He also coached in San Diego and will coach in Washington in 2006.

THE MOOSE

Mike Marshall had only 25 at-bats as a September call-up, but earned a spot on the Dodgers' division series roster after Ron Cey was sidelined with a fractured left forearm. The righthanded hitter from Buffalo Grove, Illinois, struck out in his only postseason at-bat against Houston and was replaced by Cey on the Dodgers' postseason roster for the NLCS and World Series.

The six-foot-five slugger was far from an organizational afterthought, though, because in 1981 he captured the Pacific Coast League Triple Crown, batting .373 with 34 homers and 137 RBI. He was named Minor League Player of the Year by Topps and *The Sporting News*. Marshall was both versatile and powerful. The only question for Mike was which position he would finally play on a regular basis—and when. He saw action at first, third, and the outfield for Los Angeles in 1981, and in his first Major League at-bat, he hit what should have been a home run, but the ball bounced in and out of the right-field pavilion so fast, it was only ruled a double by the umpire. Marshall, nicknamed "Moose" for his size, was an All-Star for L.A. in 1984, batting .257 with 21 homers in 134 games. But he came into his own the following year, as he hit .293 with 28 homers and 95 RBI.

The former high school All-American went on to play 11 Major League seasons, nine for the Dodgers. Now 46, Marshall is the manager of the El Paso Diablos, an independent Minor League baseball team. Marshall's roster is largely comprised of minor-league veterans and players hoping to impress scouts from Major League affiliates, so Marshall's job is largely instructive and developmental in nature.

The 1981 championship was especially sweet to me after nearly having my career cut short by an Achilles tendon injury two years earlier.

SAVING OLD GLORY
AND THE NLCS TOO

I played 19 years in the Major Leagues, but I'm probably remembered as much for saving a flag as winning one. Perhaps best known for snatching an American flag from two would-be flag burners during a game in 1976, I was traded to the Dodgers prior to 1977 and spent my final eight seasons with Los Angeles. In 1981 I hit 11 homers with 25 RBI in 130 at-bats. I was mostly a reserve in the 1981 regular season, which I finished with the best on-base percentage (.423) and slugging average (.608) on the club. But my regular-season accomplishments paled in comparison to the pennant-winning home run I hit in Game 5 of the NLCS, a blow that gave us a 2-1 win in Montreal and a ticket to the World Series.

I'd say my best season came with the Cubs in 1976, when I hit 32 homers. But of course, nothing compares to winning a championship, so 1981 is one of my most cherished years in the Majors. While I was still a player, I worked for KABC-TV as a sportscaster during the Dodgers' offseasons. Today I'm one of the Dodgers' broadcasters.

BUFF MAKES THE BIGS

A year to the day after Los Angeles inked Tom Niedenfuer to his first professional contract, the hard-throwing righty was called up to the Major Leagues when Rick Sutcliffe went on the disabled list with a torn arch in his right foot. The following day—August 15, 1981— Niedenfuer made his Major League debut. There was no doubt about his fastball when he was called up, he just needed some confidence, like every other rookie to ever come up to the big leagues. We called him "Buff," short for buffalo. He was a big (six foot five, 225 pounds), lovable kid with all the tools to be a good relief pitcher.

In his first professional confrontation, he struck out Atlanta's Bob Horner on three pitches. He picked up his first win two days later, pitching two scoreless innings. Out of the bullpen, he went 3-1 in 17

As with most young players, Tom Niedenfuer just needed confidence in himself. He got all the encouragement he needed from his teammates, who saw the rich talent he had.

appearances over the season's final month and a half. In the postseason, he appeared in four games and did not allow an earned run.

In the 1981 World Series, he pitched three scoreless innings of relief in Game 1 and also pitched two frames in the Dodgers' Game 4 win. Armed with a 94 miles-per-hour sinking fastball, Niedenfuer spent five full seasons with the Dodgers and 10 years in the Majors, finishing with a 3.29 ERA and posting double-digit save totals in six consecutive years. His finest season came with the Dodgers in 1983, when he was 8-3 with 11 saves and a 1.90 ERA. But he will forever be remembered as the pitcher who served up Jack Clark's three-run homer that eliminated the Dodgers from the 1985 NL Championship Series.

A DOCTOR'S EXCUSE

Alejandro Peña made his big-league debut in 1981 with 14 appearances for the Dodgers, recording two saves. He was sharp in the NLCS, allowing only one hit in 2⅓ innings, but did not appear in our other postseason series for a very good reason: He collapsed in the shower after the first World Series game in New York with what eventually was diagnosed as a bleeding ulcer. We had to try to pick him up, wet and with soap all over his body, to get him into the training room.

Peña would get his chance for a larger role in future seasons, earning the win in the first game of the 1988 World Series—the game Kirk Gibson won with his dramatic pinch-hit homer off Dennis Eckersley. Peña made five trips to the postseason in 15 big-league seasons, finishing with a 2.01 career ERA in the playoffs.

While Peña spent most of his career as a reliever, he was a member of the Dodgers' starting rotation in 1983 and 1984. He turned in a 2.75 ERA in 1983, good for fifth in the league, and led the NL with a 2.48 mark in 1984. Peña spent eight full seasons with the Dodgers and also pitched for the Mets, Braves, Pirates, Red Sox, and Marlins.

His blazing fastball helped him record a 3.11 career ERA and five seasons of 11 or more saves. Today, Peña lives in Roswell, Georgia.

BIG BIRD ROOSTS IN L.A.

Of all the guys who migrated to the Dodgers around this time, Jerry Reuss was the one who probably benefited the most from a change of teams. Those of us who had faced him while he was with other teams already knew of the immense talent he possessed. What we weren't sure of was whether "Big Bird" knew how good he could be. As we learned, he did know, and he wanted to be even better. He is bright, articulate, and focused.

Reuss was lights-out in the regular season of 1981, turning in a 2.30 ERA, and he kept it going in the postseason. He threw nine shutout innings in the Dodgers' Game 2 playoff loss to Houston—a game that was eventually won by the Astros in the 11th inning— before winning the NLDS clincher against Nolan Ryan with another nine innings of shutout ball. The six-foot-five lefty lost his only start in the NLCS as well as Game 1 of the World Series, but he rebounded for a complete-game victory in Game 5, allowing only one run.

Reuss helped pitch us to our first-half division title, turning in a 5-2 record and 1.89 ERA prior to the work stoppage. But he also will be remembered for suffering a leg injury during a workout the day before Opening Day, forcing manager Tommy Lasorda to turn to an unproven and generally unknown lefthander by the name of Fernando Valenzuela to open the season.

Reuss spent 22 years in the Major Leagues, including nine with Los Angeles, and he never recorded a lower ERA than he did in 1981. He led the Dodgers in wins (18) and posted a 2.51 ERA in 1980, and also threw a no-hitter in San Francisco, earning NL Comeback Player of the Year after posting a 7-14 record in 1979. All those accomplishments in 1980 came after Reuss began the season in the bullpen. But when Dave Goltz missed his May 16 start with the flu and Rick Sutcliffe struggled with his control, Reuss stepped in and

For all of the attention Fernando Valenzuela received and deserved, we probably wouldn't have succeeded if Jerry Reuss had not become a dominant left-handed starting pitcher in 1981.

became a permanent fixture in the rotation. He went 12-2 against pennant-contenders Houston, Cincinnati, Montreal, and Pittsburgh, foreshadowing his success in the clutch during our world championship season.

Reuss won 10 or more games 12 times in his career and finished 220-191 with a 3.64 ERA. Although he never played college ball—he went directly to the minors after the Cardinals drafted him out of high school—Reuss attended classes at Southern Illinois University, Central Missouri State, and UC Santa Barbara during his playing career. Presently, he resides in Las Vegas.

THE INSTIGATOR

Shortstop Bill Russell suffered a slew of injuries in 1981 and turned in one of his worst offensive seasons, although he continued to play effective defense. His righthanded bat came alive in the playoffs, however, when he batted .263. Russell knocked an RBI single in our 2-1 win in Game 4 of the Division Series and he had two hits in Games 3 and 6 of the World Series.

If the hits were sparse during the regular season, Russell made them count as best he could, delivering back-to-back game-winning hits against the Astros on April 11 and April 12. He recorded his 1,500th hit on September 8, 1981, against the Giants.

Russell played all of his 18 Major League seasons for the Dodgers, retiring after 1986 with a .263 average and nearly 2,000 hits. A converted centerfielder, Russell had his finest season in 1978, batting a career-best .286 with 32 doubles, a Dodger record for a shortstop. Coach Monty Basgall was the man responsible for converting Russell and Lopes from outfielders to infielders.

If you didn't see him play every day, you probably missed just how good Russell was. He was regarded by most of his teammates as one of the best clutch hitters on the team, and was a .294 career hitter in the postseason. Not much of a power hitter, Russell didn't hit a ball out of the park in 1981 and registered zero home runs in six of his

Bill Russell, an All-Star shortstop, was considered by teammates to be the best hitter on the club with a game on the line. *Focus on Sport/Getty Images*

Major League seasons, including the final three of his career. However, he was an outstanding contact hitter, striking out once every 11.7 plate appearances over his career.

He was a feisty player, too—one of the biggest instigators on the club. Lasorda used to say that "Ropes," as Russell was called, had started at least 20 fights during his career—but hadn't been in one yet! The three-time All-Star never won a Gold Glove due to some relatively high error totals, but he displayed above-average range throughout his career and was considered a good glove man.

A Kansas prep basketball star, Russell was selected by Los Angeles in the ninth round of the 1966 draft. He displayed a flair for the dramatic right off the bat, as he hit for the cycle in his Dodger debut in 1969. Currently, Russell tries to keep the drama to a minimum, serving as an Umpires Observer for Major League Baseball.

MAKE ROOM FOR SAXY

Steve Sax made his big-league debut in 1981, playing regularly after being called up on August 18 when Davey Lopes went on the disabled list with torn fibers in his groin. Sax singled in his first Major League at-bat and hit his first home run five days later, looking comfortable at age 21 at the game's highest level. His .277 average and unbridled energy earned him a place on the Dodgers' roster for all three postseason series, although he received only one playoff at-bat. Despite the time spent in the Majors, Sax still earned Player of the Year honors in the Texas League, where he batted .346 with 34 steals and 94 runs in 115 games.

Sax was an aggressive player who modeled his game after that of Pete Rose. He made further strides in 1982, when he captured the NL Rookie of the Year award and made the All-Star team by batting .282 and stealing 49 bases. He would go on to be named to five All-Star teams in his career, three with the Dodgers. He won the NL Silver Slugger award in 1986, batting a career-best .332 (second in the

league) while totaling more walks than strikeouts. After eight years in
Los Angeles, Sax went on to play for the Yankees, White Sox, and A's.
"Saxy" was a bit hyper, but a breath of fresh air with his
enthusiasm. He came up and showed why scouts were high on him:
he could run, hit, and field. The future of the Dodgers would include
Steve Sax at second base. Steve just needed playing time ... and maybe
a few Valium. His problems throwing to first wouldn't develop into an
issue until later on. Those struggles began in 1983, when he
committed 30 errors. Unlike many who've faced the same mental
block, though, Sax overcame it and was able to play his entire career
at second base. In 1989, he led AL second basemen in fielding and
double plays. He retired at age 34 with a .281 career average and
1,949 hits, and now lives in Roseville, California, where he is an
investment advisor.

A YOUNG BACKSTOP

Mike Scioscia won the starting catcher's job from Steve Yeager and
Joe Ferguson in his first full season with the Dodgers in 1981 as a 22-
year-old. He hit .270 at the plate that season, striking out only once
every 16.1 at-bats. In a platoon role with Yeager, the left-handed
Scioscia played nearly every day because the Dodgers faced so few
lefthanded pitchers.

Scioscia's brightest moment of 1981 came in Game 1 of the
NLCS, when he hit a home run at Dodger Stadium with his parents
in attendance. He stepped to the plate only five times in the World
Series as the Dodgers went with the veteran Yeager, who responded by
hitting two home runs. But the future belonged to Scioscia, who went
on to a solid 13-year career with the Dodgers.

The former first-round pick made two All-Star teams and
established himself as a strong defensive backstop, earning Dodgers
vice president Al Campanis's praise for blocking the plate better than
any catcher Campanis had ever seen. Scioscia studied the science of

Mike Scioscia was a protégé of Hall of Fame catcher Roy Campanella, and he learned his lessons well. He was the youngest starter in the lineup when the season opened.

catching with one of the great professors, three-time MVP Roy Campanella.

Although he was not known for power, "Sciosh" was a reliable contact hitter who delivered one of the most dramatic home runs in Dodger history—a game-tying blast off Doc Gooden in the ninth inning to send a 1988 NLCS game into extra innings and avoid imminent elimination. While he batted only .259 in his career, Scioscia consistently ranked among the league leaders in at-bats per strikeout and compiled a .344 career on-base percentage. His best season came in 1985, when he batted a career-best .296 with 53 RBI, 77 walks, and just 21 strikeouts.

After his playing career drew to a close, Scioscia entered the coaching world. Named manager of the Angels prior to the 2000 season, he has established himself as one of the best skippers in the AL, and already has a World Series ring as a manager after the Angels won it all in 2002. Former Dodgers Alfredo Griffin, Mickey Hatcher, and Ron Roenicke currently serve on his coaching staff.

NOT A GOOD LOSER

Reggie Smith was traded to the Dodgers in 1976 and was at the tail end of his career during our world championship run, but he came through as a pinch-hitter during the playoffs, going 2-for-4, with an RBI in our Game 4 win in the NLCS. Smith had shoulder surgery in September 1980, cutting short an All-Star season in which he batted .322 with 15 homers in 92 games. In 1981, though, a hobbled Smith did not make a single start. Thirty-one of his 35 at-bats came as a pinch hitter, and Smith responded with six pinch-hits for eight RBI, including a double and a homer.

He was as intense a player as I have ever been associated with. The phrase "good loser" has never crossed his lips—nor will it, ever! Reggie was driven to win. Losing, to put it simply, was never an option. When healthy, he was as fearsome a hitter and outfielder as you will find. The switch-hitter made three of his seven All-Star teams with the

Dodgers, turning in two of the best power seasons of his career. He clubbed a career-best 32 homers in 1977 while leading the league in on-base percentage, and added 29 homers and a .295 average the next year.

Smith joined the Giants as a free agent in 1982, the final season of a 17-year career, and batted a more characteristic .284 with 18 homers in 106 games. Reggie spent his first ten seasons with the Red Sox and Cardinals and totaled 2,020 hits in his career, including 314 home runs. He currently lives in Woodland Hills, California, where he runs the Reggie Smith Baseball Academy.

PRE-FAME "STEW"

Dave Stewart was initially cut from the Dodgers prior to 1981, as he was out of options and ticketed for Triple-A, but management reversed its decision and released Don Stanhouse instead. Stewart rewarded the Dodgers' confidence with a blazing start, going 4-1 with three saves and 1.00 ERA in his first 17 games. He finished the season with a 2.49 ERA. Pitching in relief in the playoffs, Stewart was charged with both of the Dodgers' losses in the Division Series, allowing three runs in two appearances. He didn't pitch in the NLCS, but rebounded to make two scoreless appearances in the World Series.

He spent parts of four seasons in Los Angeles as a reliable pitcher, before being traded to the Rangers for Rick Honeycutt in August of 1983. He struggled in Texas and later in Philadelphia, but was rejuvenated in 1986 when he joined Oakland midway through the year and went 9-5. Stewart won at least 20 games in each of the next four seasons, and finished in the top four of Cy Young Award voting each year. His brilliant span was highlighted by a 21-9 record and 3.32 ERA during his lone All-Star season in 1989.

That year Stewart pitched brilliantly in the playoffs and earned World Series MVP honors as Oakland won it all. One year later, he earned ALCS MVP honors with the A's, an award he'd win again in 1993 with the Blue Jays, who went on to a world championship.

Without a radar gun, you wouldn't think "Stew" was throwing as hard as he was, thanks to good mechanics and a fluid delivery. One of the really hard workers in the game, he was always inquisitive and wanted to learn more about his craft. The Oakland native finished his career 168-129, but always saved his finest moments for the postseason. In 11 postseason series, Stewart was 10-6 with a 2.84 ERA. Today he works as an agent for Major League players.

CONFRONTING LASORDA

Rick Sutcliffe won 17 games for the Dodgers in 1979 as a 23-year-old and was Rookie of the Year, but control problems derailed him in 1980 as his ERA ballooned from 3.46 in 1979 to 5.56 in 1980. He pitched sparingly in 1981, making only 14 appearances, six of them starts.

The six-foot-seven righthander opened the season in the rotation, but was bounced after six starts, despite a 3.48 ERA. He battled nagging injuries and pitched only once in August and twice in September. Getting passed over for a start in September triggered a legendary showdown in manager Tommy Lasorda's office. Sutcliffe later said he picked up Lasorda by the uniform collar. Not surprisingly, Sutcliffe was left off the postseason roster and was traded to the Indians following the season. It was a move the Dodgers would come to regret, as Sutcliffe went 14-8 with a 2.96 ERA in 1982 and totaled 51 wins over the next three seasons.

A big, hard thrower with a ton of guts, "Sut" was never mistaken for a wallflower. He had one thing going for him right away too: He wasn't afraid to challenge hitters and didn't back away, even if he made a mistake with a pitch. He was a very quick learner.

Finishing with a 171-139 career record, Sutcliffe was a three-time All-Star and won the 1984 NL Cy Young Award by virtue of his 16-1 record with the Cubs after a June trade from Cleveland. Although Chicago dropped the NLCS to the Padres that year, it wasn't because of Sutcliffe, who was 1-1 with a 3.38 ERA and also went 3-for-6 with a home run at the plate. After retiring, Sutcliffe found his way behind the microphone, and presently serves as a broadcaster for the Padres and ESPN.

MR. EVERYWHERE

Derrel Thomas, the Dodgers' "Mr. Everywhere," saw action everywhere but pitcher, catcher, and first base in 1981. If you needed a sink fixed, you'd call a plumber. If you needed a guy to play eight different positions, you'd call Derrel. "D.T." drove Lasorda nuts. Tommy hated the "basket catch" with a passion—and Derrel knew it! If a ball was hit his way he would see how close to the ground he could catch it, and then watch Tommy go nuts in the dugout.

The lefthanded hitter had several highlights during the 1981 regular season, including a game-winning home run on August 22 and a three-hit game on September 6 that included a great leaping catch at shortstop. He drove in 15 runs prior to the strike in only 106 at-bats, and led all reserves in games and at-bats during the regular season. He appeared in 11 playoff games, mostly as a pinch-hitter, pinch-runner, and defensive replacement. He scored five runs in the playoffs, despite a 1-for-10 batting line.

Thomas came to the Dodgers midway through his 15-year career as the second free agent ever signed by the team. He was never a standout, but his versatility helped him play in 1,597 games for seven different teams. The Los Angeles native particularly enjoyed playing for the Dodgers for five seasons, considering it was a boyhood dream come true. Thomas, a Dorsey High School standout as a pitcher and shortstop, frequented Dodger Stadium in his youth, when he idolized Willie Davis and Maury Wills (whose No. 30 he wore with the Dodgers). His enthusiasm was reflected in his play and flashy on-field demeanor.

After his playing career ended, Thomas became a popular high school coach before he pleaded no contest to cocaine charges in 1992 and spent 47 days in jail. Today, Thomas works with Baseballers

Derrel Thomas' defensive versatility and speed provided Tommy Lasorda with the flexibility managers need to win championships.

Against Drugs, as well as his own non-profit organization, the California Winter League, which teaches baseball fundamentals to children ages 7-18.

A ROOKIE SEASON TO REMEMBER

Fernando Valenzuela made his Dodger debut as a September call-up from Double-A in 1980, and proceeded to pitch 17⅔ scoreless innings of relief to close out the season. As impressive as that brief introduction was, though, it didn't prepare Los Angeles for what the 20-year-old would accomplish in 1981. In his strike-shortened rookie season, Valenzuela won 13 games while leading the Majors in shutouts and strikeouts, becoming the first player ever to win Rookie of the Year and the Cy Young Award in the same season. His 36-inning scoreless streak was the longest in the NL and was accompanied by scoreless streaks of 32⅔ innings and 18 innings (twice). Named Major League Player of the Year by *The Sporting News*, Valenzuela also was no slouch at the plate. He hit .250 and drove in seven runs, earning him the Silver Slugger award for being the best-hitting pitcher in the NL.

Thrust into the Opening Day start when Jerry Reuss pulled a muscle, Valenzuela pitched like an ace most of the season. He threw complete games in seven of his first eight starts, posting a 0.50 ERA during that stretch and igniting Fernandomania in Los Angeles. Valenzuela started the 1981 All-Star game for the NL, throwing a scoreless inning, and finished the season with a 2.48 ERA. He was equally comfortable on the postseason stage, where he went 1-0 with a 1.06 ERA in two Division Series starts, 1-1 with a 2.40 ERA in the NLCS, and tossed a complete-game win in his only World Series start.

Valenzuela went on to have a 17-year career in the Majors, including 11 seasons with the Dodgers. He won 21 games in 1986 and threw more than 250 innings for six consecutive seasons. "El Toro" completed 20 games in 1986, making him the last Major Leaguer—perhaps ever—to complete that many starts in a season.

Better check his ID. Fernando Valenzuela was only 20 years old his rookie season, but he pitched as if he'd been through it all before.

After being released by the Dodgers during spring training of 1991, Valenzuela won only 17 games over the next five years and pitched in Mexico during 1992. He enjoyed a couple of nice comeback seasons with the Padres, though, going 21-11 combined in 1995-1996.

The screwball specialist from Mexico did not speak English when he joined the Dodgers. Today he makes his living behind the microphone, serving as an analyst on the Dodgers' Spanish-language broadcasts.

WELCHY

Bob Welch didn't expect to pitch at all in 1981, as a bone spur in his right elbow put him on the verge of surgery during spring training. However, rest and medication returned him to the mound, and Welch went on to make 23 starts that year. He won his last four decisions of the season, and went 5-2 with a 3.75 ERA after the work stoppage. But in the playoffs, he served mostly as a reliever, with the exception of a start in Game 4 of the World Series. He was pulled in the game after allowing three hits and a walk without recording an out.

"Welchy" was one of our favorites. Bobby was a baseball player first and a pitcher second. He loved the game and he showed great resiliency on the mound, never resorting to excuses. He was his own harshest critic.

Welch, a first-round draft pick by the Dodgers in 1977, broke into the bigs the following year at age 21, going 7-4 with a 2.03 ERA. His performance led Lasorda to compare him with Don Drysdale. He hooked up in an unforgettable confrontation with Reggie Jackson in the 1977 World Series, eventually striking out the slugger to conclude a tense showdown. Alcoholism hindered his performance in 1979, however, but over the offseason Welch spent a month at a treatment center and responded by winning 14 games and making the All-Star team in 1980.

Welch spent the first 10 years of his career with Los Angeles, pitching effectively but never winning more than 16 games. With Oakland, he earned a Cy Young Award in a magical 1990 season when he won 27 games against just six losses with a 2.95 ERA. He finished his career with 211 wins and a 3.47 ERA. He is now back in a Dodger uniform, serving as the pitching coach for Rookie-level Ogden. Prior to that, Welch was the pitching coach for the Diamondbacks when the team captured its 2001 World Championship, and for Arizona State.

MY BUD BOOMER

Talking about Steve Yeager puts me into dangerous territory. Steve and I were roommates for a few years during spring training and occasionally on the road during the season. We have laughed together, cried together, and been there for one another for a lot of years. He is one of a kind, and the best friend anyone could have.

Yeager could flat-out catch! He was quick as a cat behind the plate with one of the best arms I've ever seen on a catcher. He threw out 7-of-20 would-be base stealers in 1981 and 32-of-70 in 1978. Despite his defensive strengths, he was almost an afterthought during the 1981 regular season as a platoon catcher, totaling only 86 at-bats as the Dodgers rarely encountered left-handed pitching. After batting .209 with three homers in the regular season, though, Yeager exploded in the playoffs. He was 2-for-5 with a double against Houston, 1-for-2 against the Expos and 4-for-14 with a double and two homers in the World Series, including the game-winner in Game 5. As a result, Yeager shared World Series MVP honors with Ron Cey and Pedro Guerrero.

"Boomer," as we called him, spent the first 14 years of his career in Los Angeles, usually serving in a part-time role. He finished his career with a .228 batting average and 102 homers, but he had a knack for starring on baseball's biggest stage as evidenced by his success in the 1981 playoffs. For his career, he hit .252 in the postseason with five home runs. In the 1977 postseason, he played in every game, going 6-for-19 with two homers and five RBI.

Yeager was also a good man to have behind the plate during the regular season. In 1974, the Dodgers won 24 of Yeager's starts in a row. Signed by the Dodgers for $8,000 three days after he graduated from high school in 1967, Yeager was married in 1976 on the steps of City Hall—with Mayor Tom Bradley as his best man. His uncle, Chuck Yeager, was the first man to break the sound barrier, although Steve wasn't a threat to repeat that feat, stealing only 14 bases in his career.

Steve Yeager's playing time was limited during the regular season, but in the postseason spotlight he was an MVP star.

Yeager was recently promoted to the role of hitting coach with the Dodgers' Triple-A team in Las Vegas, and I'm sure he'll be back in the Major Leagues before too long. He managed the independent Long Beach Breakers for two seasons beginning in 2000, guiding them to a Western League crown in his first year.

Now that you've met the team, it's time to rally the troops and head to spring training. Dodgertown, here we come!

3

DESTINATION: DODGERTOWN

Every year, Major League Baseball teams pack their bags and head off for six weeks of spring training in either Florida or Arizona. They check into hotels and individually travel to and from their training facilities every day, and then fend for themselves in finding restaurants each night after workouts. They arrange for rental cars, find grocery stores, cleaners, and theaters.

But it is different with the Dodgers, and it has been for more than half a century, which I feel is one of the reasons the Dodgers have established a "family atmosphere" and allowed players to bond with one another both on and off the field. Once the Dodgers arrive in Vero Beach, Florida, they have everything they need right where they are.

It was a visionary decision by Branch Rickey to take the advice of a local businessman, Bud Holman, and move the Dodgers' spring training camp to the abandoned barracks of a WWII Naval fighter-training base in Vero Beach. It was a move as brilliant as it was bold. At its peak, "Dodgertown" housed upwards of 650 Major and Minor League players.

Over the years, the facilities at Dodgertown have accommodated the change in the game and the franchise. The old naval-base barracks have been replaced with single-story bungalows and a main office staffed 24 hours a day. There is a large dining room to feed players and staff, a six-bed medical center, a laundry and cleaners, movies every night, pool tables, ping pong, a swimming pool, tennis courts, and three fishing lakes. One of the lakes was even designed by Walter O'Malley in the shape of a heart, for his wife, Kay. Until recent years, there were also two golf courses, all located inside the 400-plus acres of the campus. The streets are even named after former Dodger greats who have trained there. The facility now serves as a conference center year-round—except for six wonderful weeks from mid-February through March.

Dodgertown offers six full practice fields, two half-diamonds, indoor batting and pitching cages, and Holman Stadium, where the spring home schedule is played. To me, it's the "Disneyland of baseball." The large banner draped across the main entrance says it all: "Dodgertown, the spring training home of the Los Angeles Dodgers … welcome home Dodgers." You see that sign driving in, and it's good to be back "home."

I didn't come up through the Dodger farm system. But Ron Cey did—and he told me that when you grew up a Dodger, you grew up a little differently than you did in other organizations.

"You become very familiar with Dodger tradition and history and the subliminal messages that were being intentionally given to you and what was expected," Cey said. "So I think one of the things about playing in the Dodger organization was that when we went to spring training, our goal was to be the world champion."

CAMP: WHAT IF?

The spring trainings tend to run together once you've sweated through a few of them, but there was a different feel at Dodgertown in 1981. For one thing, even before spring training, there were storm clouds. Ominous rhetoric was volleyed between representatives of owners and the Players Association over compensation for free agency that would disintegrate into a strike.

More immediately, there was uncertainty in the opinion of manager Tommy Lasorda whether the club that reported to Florida still had what it took to be a champion. General manager Al Campanis had pretty much stood pat in the offseason, bringing back essentially the same club that just missed the postseason in 1980. Lasorda labeled spring training that season, "Camp: What If?," saying the team would be a contender, *if*: Reggie Smith, Bill Russell, Davey Lopes, Don Stanhouse, and Terry Forster could recover from injuries; Fernando Valenzuela was for real or Rick Sutcliffe could regain his rookie-of-the-year form in hopes that one of them could replace Don Sutton in the starting rotation; Dave Goltz could regain his ace ability from his time with the Twins; Pedro Guerrero was ready to be the big-time player his skills indicated he would become.

But if unrest off the field accompanied training camp, so did the promise of a handful of up-and-comers like Guerrero, Mike Scioscia and, of course, Valenzuela, who surprised most of baseball but not the man who acquired him.

"He has the chance to be a star," Campanis said even before spring training started, and well before Fernandomania broke out.

From the players' viewpoint, this spring training was different because of an unmistakable sense of urgency. This was a veteran club that for too long had been viewed as an underachiever. The Dodgers had gone to the World Series in 1977 and 1978, but lost both times to the Yankees, just as the Brooklyn Dodgers used to do with regularity. Then in 1979, injuries left us a shell of those two previous squads. And in 1980, we took the Houston Astros to a sudden-death playoff game, but lost it.

Now we were getting a little long in the tooth as a team, and when we got to Florida, nobody really knew whether this might be our last chance as a group to reach the Promised Land. But I think everybody sensed it. And if we didn't, we weren't paying attention. Because all we had to do was look at the kids who were getting increasing playing time in those spring games: Scioscia, Guerrero, Steve Sax, Mike Marshall, Candy Maldonado, etc. They were here to replace us—the only question was, when?

OPENING THE MAIL

Lasorda reinforced the sense of urgency he wished to place upon the 1981 season before we even reported to Dodgertown.

"I wrote a letter to every player in the offseason," Lasorda recalls. "I told the guys to be in the best shape of their life when they got to Florida, because I really believed we were going to win this thing and go all the way. We had a lot of talent, but to go all the way, we had to be willing to pay the price.

"I'll tell you how talented this team was, or at least how talented it thought it was. One day we were playing the Reds in spring training and they had a lefthander on the mound, Charlie Leibrandt, and he was just mowing us down. Even though it was a spring game, I was furious. I mean, I was going nuts in the dugout, and finally Reggie Smith came up to me and said, 'Take it easy, Tommy. We want this guy (Leibrandt) to make the club.' And you know what? He did make the club, and when the games counted, we lathered him. That was the kind of confidence that club had."

Tommy repeated the message from that letter when he addressed the club before the opening workout. My roomie, catcher Steve Yeager, had heard it all from Lasorda over the years, but he sensed this time there was something different—Tommy really meant it.

"Tommy realized, as did everybody else, that there were some kids down on the farm that were knocking at the door, and I think that Tommy knew, sooner or later, all the guys he'd had since '77 were going to be departing," Yeager says. "I think it was a little more of a challenge that Tommy put out there on us and, you know, we did what we had to do."

Tommy Lasorda challenged his team in the spring. But, he personally rose to the occasion during the season, in what many believe was his finest managing performance in a Hall of Fame career.

Jerry Reuss, another of my closest friends on that club, had gone through the toughest of times with the Pittsburgh Pirates before he was traded to the Dodgers prior to the 1979 season. He also remembers Lasorda's speech in 1981.

"I always viewed Tommy, in that meeting in particular, as one of the greatest salesmen. Like the old joke, he was a guy who could've sold ice cubes to Eskimos," says Reuss. "Many of his addresses to the team were motivational, but they were also challenging to the guys, in such a way as to bring out the best in them, not challenging anything else as far as their fortitude and their drive and their abilities, but he wanted to get the best out of everybody.

"Out of all the managers I had, Tommy had more meetings because Tommy liked to address guys. He preferred a lot of one on one and was hands on, as far as his managing technique. A lot of managers just let guys go because players are professionals and know how to go about their business. Whether that's right, whether that's wrong, it was just Tommy's personal preference to have a lot of meetings. He was able to get most of the guys on that team to play as close to their maximum as he possibly could. He was a bit upset about the fact that we were so close in 1980 and we lost it on the last day. He believed that we were still the best team in our division. And this might be our last chance to prove it."

THE INFIELD

Nobody felt the urgency more than shortstop Bill Russell, the dean of this club, who made his Major League debut in 1969 and now was in his third decade, still looking for his first World Series ring.

"We felt like a band of brothers," Russell says. "We were there so long and we accomplished so many things, but one thing eluded us and that's a world championship. We'd been there a couple times and we'd had opportunities, but we just couldn't get that championship. It seemed like the Yankees, they were playing so well in those days that they were always there along with us.

Davey Lopes, Bill Russell, Steve Garvey, and Ron Cey: four players, one infield, 8½ seasons. I doubt baseball will ever see anything like that again.

"And we knew Steve Sax was coming up, and you'd always hear how well he was doing and he was going to be the next player to come up and take one of our places. He played second base, where Davey Lopes had played almost a decade. Not that we talked about it, but we knew that this was probably our last opportunity—after being there over eight years together—to win a championship ring together. And we finally pulled it off, but it wasn't easy. I guess if you could map it out, you wouldn't do it any differently, other than the strike. But the way we went about it, we finally accomplished the ultimate dream."

Russell referred to "eight years together." The number actually is 8½, and Dodger fans know what 8½ means. That's how many seasons the infield of Steve Garvey, Lopes, Russell, and Ron Cey played together. Nowadays, with the way free agency has turned players into vagabonds, an infield remaining intact that long is unthinkable. But back then, it was the culmination of the great Dodger drafts of the late 1960s and the developmental farm system that formed the core of that 1981 Dodger team. They played for Lasorda in the Minor Leagues, had pretty much come up together to the Major Leagues, and once there demonstrated a cohesiveness that helped the total exceed the sum of the individuals.

While some people would argue that the record-setting infield of the Dodgers may not have included the slickest, fastest, or even the best at their individual positions, I am still convinced that they were the most consistent group of infielders in the game at that time. Because of their tenure together, each one of them knew exactly where the other one was going to be on a given play, and how they would react to just about any situation. They didn't always make the play, but they always came back on the next play with an idea of what to do with the ball if it was hit to them. All Lasorda had to do was just keep writing their names onto the lineup card.

"Tommy had a way of knowing how to motivate each of us," recalls Russell. "He had us all in the Minor Leagues, he knew how to handle us. But the bottom line is, we came to play. It was pretty easy for Tommy to make out a lineup with the four of us out there just about every day, and very seldom did any of us get hurt. When we came to the ballpark each day, the feeling was, if our team stayed close to the opponent, with the talent we had, we were going to beat you. It was just a special feeling that we had about each other. It's hard to describe. It was something that we earned because we worked hard to get where we were, but we knew the end result: we were going to beat you."

TEED OFF

Some of us spent a lot of time in the spring together at Dodger Pines Country Club, playing golf and talking baseball. With the 18-hole and 9-hole courses right there at Dodgertown (they're gone now), what better way to work out the kinks and soreness of a long day of practice or a game than with a round of golf? Tommy didn't like golf very much and thought it was a waste of time, so he put in some rules for the golf courses. No golf until 3 p.m., and no golf carts—you walked the course or you would be fined and barred from the course for a week.

The tradition of the Dodgers "family" was reinforced each spring on the golf courses when veteran players would ask a couple rookies or minor leaguers out to play. The topic of discussion was always baseball during those afternoon trips to the course. We talked about tradition and winning, commitment and improving, believing in one's self, and becoming mentally strong. All the things that go hand in hand with being a winning organization and passing the baton to the next generation of Dodger players. Those trips to the golf course set the Dodger organization apart from the rest. Not only did they cause the players to bond, but they also worked wonders for lowering handicaps.

So while Dodgertown was designed for work, recreation wasn't shunned and laughter was encouraged. Especially by Lasorda, who felt it was his job to keep the atmosphere loose. And the players usually cooperated. Or maybe the word is instigated. Like the time early in the 1981 camp when Lasorda tumbled out of the passenger side of a golf cart that took a turn too fast. Reggie Smith, claiming concern for his manager's safety, buckled Lasorda in with a safety belt made out of a bicycle chain tied to one of the cart's posts. To ensure the chain did the trick, he locked it with a padlock, which had no key. Equipment manager Nobe Kawano had to be summoned to free Lasorda, who—for some reason—failed to see the humor.

TWEAKING THE ROSTER

There was nothing funny about the health of the pitching staff with one week left in spring training. Bob Welch's elbow flared up, as it did annually. Dave Goltz had a sore groin. Terry Forster's elbow wasn't 100 percent. Forster didn't think there was anything humorous about being called into Lasorda's office to be told he was being released. He still wasn't laughing when told it was April Fools' Day and he was the designated fool.

Nobody was laughing about the uncertainty over Reggie Smith's shoulder and Pedro Guerrero's readiness for the Major Leagues, which prompted Campanis to trade popular utilityman Mickey Hatcher and two Minor Leaguers to the Minnesota Twins for outfielder Ken Landreaux a week before Opening Day. That satisfied Campanis's desire to add a left-handed bat to the lineup. Over the winter, Campanis made an unsuccessful run at free agent Fred Lynn. In the spring he tried to package Hatcher to the Chicago Cubs for Bill Buckner, but the deal unraveled when Dodger pitching prospect Joe Beckwith, a key to the Cubs trade, had to leave camp with recurring vision problems and couldn't be added to the deal.

Smith's surgically repaired shoulder wasn't ready to throw a baseball full speed, but he hadn't completely lost his power, as he proved on getaway day from Dodgertown, when he decked a heckler outside the press room. That wouldn't be the last punch Reggie threw during that year, either.

ELEPHANT IN THE ROOM

Even though we had work to accomplish on the baseball fields to get ready for the season, there continued to be a sense of frustration hovering nearby. It was impossible to ignore, and centered on the looming summer showdown between the owners and the union over the Collective Bargaining Agreement. The Players Association needed to get the message out on the state of negotiations with the owners, and do it with every team during the few weeks of spring training. The daunting task of delivering that message fell squarely upon the shoulders of Marvin Miller, the Players Association director. So Marvin sought to address every team in Florida and Arizona.

Over the years I had come to respect and admire Miller in the way he conducted himself during times of pressure. I had my first look at him in action while serving on the American League Pension Committee while still playing with the Oakland A's in the late '60s. In the hardest of times, I never heard Miller raise his voice in anger, and he was as focused as any person I've ever been around. Players of the past, present, and future should all know Marvin Miller's great importance to each and every one of us. I'm very glad he was on our side of the table for all of those years.

I don't believe that many people outside of baseball knew then—or even now—what the issues at hand really were. To be very honest, some players didn't even know, and more disturbing, some didn't even care. One of the reasons I relinquished the position of player representative a few years prior while still with the Chicago Cubs was for that very reason. I was happy to be a "player rep," but "babysitting" simply wasn't in the job profile.

Jerry Reuss was the Dodger "rep," and a darn good one. He would need to be, especially this year. Jerry proved he was a good one at Dodgertown when, during a players meeting, he called out one player in particular who had his back to the roomful of teammates, busily rearranging stuff in his locker and not the least bit interested in the latest updates on the negotiations.

The real issues were simple for the players. The owners desperately wanted to once again rein in the players on free agency by attaching compensation that would have a chilling effect on clubs taking players from each other. The end result would discourage teams from purchasing free agents. The compensation for signing a free agent was that the signing team would have to offer up a player from its roster to send to the team losing the free agent. (Excluded from the selection were 12 "protected" players.) The Players Association maintained that any form of compensation would undermine the value of free agents. After fighting for years to obtain free-agent status, the players were not about to give an inch back at the bargaining table.

NO SUBWAY SERIES HERE

The routine of day games in Florida abruptly changed with the Freeway Series, played nearly every year between the Dodgers and the neighboring Angels in Anaheim. What better way for two teams to orchestrate their final tuneups for the regular season than to play at least a couple of night games in Major League stadiums? Whoever thought up this promotional series years ago was brilliant. It also gave the fans an official preview of their teams.

That year we won the Friday night opener, 4-1, at Anaheim Stadium, in front of a crowd of 48,331, then a stadium record. Apparently, the fans hadn't been turned off by the drumbeat of labor strife. Every one of the field-level seats, priced at $5.50 each, was sold. The Saturday crowd for an Angels win in Orange County jumped to 58,353, an indication that the fans were ready for baseball, whether the industry was ready to play or not.

We won the rubber game Sunday at Dodger Stadium behind a pair of Pedro Guerrero home runs. After the game, Lasorda named Guerrero to the starting outfield, allowing Reggie Smith more time to heal and providing Guerrero the opportunity he needed to establish himself as an everyday player. The influx of youthful talent didn't stop there, however. Mike Scioscia won the starting catching job, and Steve Howe would once again be a key part of the bullpen. We were, however, about to witness a youthful display unlike anything any of us had ever seen.

4

PLAY BALL!

Opening Day for a player is like the Fourth of July, a movie premiere for a film you starred in, and the birth of your child all rolled into a five- to six-hour window. Friends and family join the media and the fans to witness the launching of the newest edition of the Dodgers. Hopefully, this new model of the Dodger Blue Ship will do more than simply float over the next six months.

First-day jitters are for real. I was fortunate to play in the Majors over 19 seasons and can honestly say I got "butterflies" of varying degrees before each and every game. But nothing compares to that unique feeling I got just prior to the start of Opening Day. It's an adrenaline overload until the first pitch is thrown, then things progress to a more tolerable level.

Ollie O'Mara, a 90-year-old former Brooklyn Dodger who had played for Wilbert Robinson from 1914 to 1919, threw out the ceremonial first pitch of the 1981 season. He had played with Casey Stengel and against Babe Ruth. He recalled the runs, the hits, and the errors in his career—seven decades earlier. You could see the twinkle in his blue eyes when he spoke about the game of baseball. That's what this great game is all about; regardless of our age, the game reaches the child residing in each and every one of us. It's too bad we don't allow that little kid to come out and play more often!

OUR WALLY PIPP

Speaking of youth, Fernando Valenzuela arrived on the scene like a Latino Joe Hardy for the stretch run in 1980. A 19-year-old out of the dusty Mexican town of Etchohuaquila, the cherubic-faced left-hander threw 17⅔ scoreless innings of relief after his surprise promotion from Double-A. But it wasn't even certain through spring training whether Valenzuela would open the 1981 season in the starting rotation. Then Jerry Reuss decided he would be Superman during the workout the day before the regular season was to open and do some extra running in the outfield. I'll let him tell the rest.

"You could say I unknowingly took one for the team," jokes Reuss. "I was in the outfield the day before my Opening Day start and I thought, 'Oh, I ran distance yesterday, and I'm going to run some sprints today, I'm going to run 20 of them.'

"Well, the warning signs were out there. In spring training, no matter how old you are or how young you are, you should back off and take a little time off each week. But I didn't do that, I felt I had to make up for lost time with the two years I sort of wasted in Pittsburgh. I had to prove that I was worthy of being a starter on this ball club.

"Being in Los Angeles was where I wanted to be, and I wanted to take full advantage of that situation, so I pushed myself and I probably pushed myself too hard, weakened the muscles, and instead of taking some time off, I just kept going and going and going and finally pulled a muscle in the workout. I was in the outfield and it was feeling a little tender and I should've come off the field. But I didn't, and it only got worse from there."

This might have been one of the most opportune injuries ever suffered in Dodger history. But at the time, who knew? Burt Hooton was already in pain with an ingrown toenail, so Tommy really didn't have a lot of options for the rotation. And to be honest about it, maybe he was still stinging a bit from the previous October, when we swept the Astros the final weekend to force a sudden-death playoff game and Tommy gave the ball to Dave Goltz instead of that chubby rookie left-hander who pitched so well at the end of the season. Although it would have been unheard of to give the ball in a do-or-die game to a 19-year-old making his first Major League start, the alternative proved disastrous.

Tommy made the right call this time. He gave the ball for the Opening Day start against the Astros to Valenzuela, even though the rookie had pitched batting practice at the previous day's workout and was shocked by the news.

CHAIN REACTION

With injuries to Reuss, Hooton, Goltz, and Terry Forster, we were pretty much out of healthy pitchers. The front office went into emergency mode and designated for assignment reliever Don Stanhouse, even though he was about to start the second season of a four-year contract. That decision meant a reprieve for rookie Dave Stewart, who earlier had been told he would be sent to Triple-A and responded by punching a clubhouse wall. But Stewart was healthier than Stanhouse, and we needed healthy arms.

"Sometimes you have to admit your mistakes," Campanis said then about cutting Stanhouse. Stanhouse had only worked 21 games in 1980 because of a series of arm troubles. We were sad to see Don leave; he had been shelved by arm troubles but he was still a part of the team and a pretty good guy to have around. There were not too many dull moments in our clubhouse with Stanhouse and Jay Johnstone. Don's nickname (one of many) was "Stan the Man

Unusual." He told the story that when he took off his baseball cap, it scared people so bad they wanted to "x-ray my hair."

The release of Stanhouse also moved Steve Howe up a notch to the top of the bullpen depth chart, and he went on to become the best lefthanded Dodger reliever since Jim Brewer.

"Letting Stanhouse go gave Howe the opportunity to step up and get it done the way he could," recalls catcher Mike Sciosica. "His emergence was the turning point for the bullpen."

THIS KID IS A ROOKIE?

We didn't know much about this Valenzuela kid. But we started to talk about him very quickly, because it looked like he had already lived this life before and was coming back in a younger body.

"Fernando was a kid. He looked like a kid, he acted like a kid, but he didn't pitch like a kid. I mean, this guy, he had an idea what he was doing all the time," recalls Baker. "That's what made everybody holler that he was older than he was.

"You could really tell that he knew what he was doing whenever he got in trouble. He would go behind the mound, rub up the ball and sort of take the air out, take a 20-second timeout and then go back to pitching. If he had his act together, he would just wind up and throw, wind up and throw, but as soon as he'd get in trouble a little bit he'd sort of take the air out of the ball.

"Two guys come to mind as guys that took the world by storm when they came in. Fernando and Mark Fidrych, the difference being that Mark didn't last as long as Fernando, because Fernando was just unbelievable. Not only was he a great pitcher, he was a great athlete. I mean, he could field his position, he could hit, and I know I saw him in the dugout one day with a Hacky Sack, kicking that sack up and down off his knee, off his foot, off his elbow, off his shoulder, off his knee, and I said, 'This guy right here, this guy is something special.'"

Baseball had no idea what was about to hit it when Fernando Valenzuela took the mound on Opening Day in 1981.

Rolling his eyes skyward during his delivery to the plate, the only rookie pitcher ever to start for the Dodgers on Opening Day befuddled the Astros, 2-0, with a five-hit, 106-pitch shutout at Dodger Stadium. Fernandomania was officially underway.

"And I'll tell you," says Baker, "he was a gifted young man. He was smart. I don't think people gave him credit for how smart he was. And I realized how smart he was, because I remember Andre Dawson, he was with Montreal then, he hit a home run off Fernando. Back then, we didn't have scouting reports like we have today, all this paperwork with matchups and tendencies and histories. We didn't have that back then but Fernando didn't need it back then. He remembered exactly what pitch he had thrown to Dawson, and threw him something different in the same situation later in the season and struck him out.

"That might not sound like something special, but we're talking about a 20-year-old rookie. Twenty-year-old rookies don't think like that in the heat of the moment. But Freddy did."

FERNANDOMANIA!

It's easy to look back on the 1981 season and, with the knowledge of how it ended, realize the importance of how it began. We got off to one of the fastest starts in Los Angeles history in 1981, and if we hadn't, with the way the season wound up being split in two because of the strike, we might have never reached the postseason. To us, the fast start was accomplished mostly with pitching and mainly through the phenomenon of Fernandomania.

"To me, Fernandomania was the most exciting period of time on my watch," says former team owner Peter O'Malley. "It was just incredible. You just look back and there was no period of time that was more exciting."

When you consider all the intangibles of a magical season, you have to think of more than just the wins and losses, more than merely the statistics. With Fernando, you need to consider the impact of his presence, how this man-child won over an entire metropolis and provided our ball club with an electrifying degree of fan support that all the marketing executives in the world couldn't create. He alone created a compelling, magical chemistry.

Hall of Fame broadcaster Vin Scully, who has called every Dodger season since 1950, recalls: "To me it went beyond a normal fan love of a player. It became, I believe, a religious experience.

"I would see Hispanic parents with little children, and I know they were spending a lot of money to come to the park. But I know they were also saying to their little child: 'See that man out there? That man came from nowhere.' To use a British writer's expression, that man came from the back of beyond. And here he is. So, if you work hard, you too can rise above.

"I really felt that fervor that you don't normally feel. There's never been anything quite like Fernandomania."

And that comment, remember, comes from the man who broadcast all four of Sandy Koufax's no-hitters.

A NATURAL IN ANY LANGUAGE

But Scully wasn't the only Dodger broadcaster who could draw comparisons to Sandy Koufax's impact and, in this unique case, Jaime Jarrin played an even larger role than the iconic Scully. Jarrin was already a star in his own right, having been the Spanish-language voice of the Dodgers for more than 20 years when Valenzuela arrived. As the dashing sidekick who translated Valenzuela's words into English, Jarrin became a celebrity beyond his imagination.

But from Jarrin's vantage point, as popular as Valenzuela became, the lefthander has never received the recognition he deserved, not only for providing a welcome distraction from the labor strife, but for making baseball accessible to an entirely new audience.

"I think Fernando created more new baseball fans than any other player in history—more than Koufax, more than Drysdale, more than Mays," says Jarrin. "Thousands of fans from Mexico and Central and Latin America, who didn't care for baseball, who were only soccer and boxing fans, became baseball fans overnight and still are to this day. Ladies and girls, men and boys. Old and young. And you see how baseball is growing in Hispanic areas today, and you have to realize that Fernando created it.

"I'll tell you how I know. Because after Fernando left the Dodgers, we had to go to Mexico to renew our radio contracts and I was afraid that with Fernando gone, the Mexican stations wouldn't want to renew. But they renewed, because they told us that the fans were now baseball fans, not just Fernando fans. That's how huge of an impact he made.

"When Fernando pitched, you had trouble getting through the entrances because they were selling so many items. It was like a religious pilgrimage. We'll never see that again. Some people tried to compare when Hideo Nomo came to us with Fernando. But there's no comparison. No way."

Longtime Los Angeles sportscaster Jim Hill, a former NFL star who has covered every sports star in Southern California for the last 30 years, said Valenzuela's impact on the city far exceeded wins and losses.

"Here in L.A.," says Hill, "once something starts that's big, it just gets bigger and bigger. And especially here, with Fernando being Latino and a big Latino population here in the L.A. area, man, it just caught fire. Then, every time he pitched, there was Mexican food up in the press box, and then he would go on the road, and he would have his own press conferences on the road, and it was just the biggest thing.

"And one of the other things about it, the guys weren't jealous of that. Teammates embraced that, because they knew that it was helping everybody get to where they wanted to go. And Fernando was so innocent and there's something really special when somebody is performing that well and also possesses an air of innocence. We all want to hug them, we all want to love them, we all want to see them do well. And part of Fernando's charm was that many people thought

I've never seen an athlete embraced by a community so completely as Fernando Valenzuela was during Fernandomania. Here he tips his cap to the Dodger Stadium crowd after pitching another shutout.

he didn't speak or understand a lot of English. Fernando understood English, and he spoke English."

At his core, Fernando was a gifted pitcher in any language.

"For me, he knew how to pitch before he ever got in the big leagues," says Yeager. "He had a good idea what was going on, and I think that was from playing in Mexico all the time and playing with some guys that were Triple-A, Major League players in the Mexican League.

"That screwball of his was very good. I go back and try to compare him with the late Jim Brewer, who had a magnificent screwball. And of course he was the one who could get right-handers out and left-handers out, it didn't make any difference.

"But Freddy had a couple different pitches. If you were looking for the screwball, he had enough on his fastball to throw it middle-in and kind of freeze you, and he had a little curveball to go with that, too, so Freddy had three pitches instead of just one specialized pitch. But I think he kind of lived and died with his screwball and, especially later on in his career, he threw it too much. I think once you get that pitch in the brain of some of the hitters, you realize that you're not going to throw that pitch that often."

Fernando never seemed overwhelmed by a situation on the field. He always knew what to do with the ball when it was hit to him, how to hit, and how to run the bases. He played the game like he had been here before and had already done it. Sometimes we would joke that it appeared like Fernando had eyes in the back of his head. If a runner took off early trying to steal third base, Fernando would just spin around and pick him off. If there was a "rookie" inside that uniform, you couldn't see it. Fernando controlled his emotions like a well-seasoned riverboat gambler holding a royal flush and just waiting for someone to raise the bet.

"Some people thought that Fernando, because he was so young, didn't realize the magnitude of what was happening. But he was very, very much aware," says Jarrin. "He might have been surprised with the results. But he was already coming off a fantastic season in the Minor Leagues (13-9, 3.10 ERA at Double-A San Antonio in 1980). Then he came up to Los Angeles in the stretch drive and pitched in 10 games without allowing a run. He had pitched two seasons in Mexico. This wasn't the first time he was successful."

MAKING IT LOOK EASY

The opening series with the Astros included the first showdown between Don Sutton and his former clubhouse combatant, Steve Garvey, who won this confrontation with a second-inning single, setting in motion a four-run rally and a 7-4 victory. Although utilityman Jay Johnstone had said during an offseason radio interview that Sutton pitched with sandpaper glued to a finger to scuff the ball, we never asked for an umpire inspection and instead let our bats do the talking. We just teed off against him, sending him to the showers in the fifth inning.

Sutton had left the Dodgers for a richer free-agent contract from the Astros, and Dodger fans booed his return, forgetting his 15 years of service for Los Angeles. The next day he was quoted in the papers saying he felt "absolutely the worst hurt [he] ever experienced in professional baseball."

We went on to sweep our postseason rivals from the previous year, as former rookies of the year Rick Sutcliffe and Steve Howe pitched and new outfielder Ken Landreaux homered in a 3-2 win. We left for Candlestick Park, and in the road opener used four pitchers—Welch, Stewart, Goltz, and Bobby Castillo—to remain unbeaten with a 4-3 win.

Valenzuela appeared quite comfortable in the chilly Bay Area climate to beat Vida Blue the next night, 7-1, in a complete-game four-hitter. The Giants run was earned, the first allowed by Valenzuela in 34⅓ Major League innings.

"It's not as easy as you think," Valenzuela told reporters after the game.

Hooton went 7⅔ innings and doubled in a pair of runs in a 4-2 win that completed another series sweep the next day. The 6-0 start represented the best for the Dodgers since the 1955 season, which ended with Brooklyn's first Dodger championship. We considered that a pretty good omen.

Ken Landreaux (sliding into home plate) was acquired from Minnesota just days before the 1981 regular season opened because Dodgers general manager Al Campanis felt the lineup needed a left-handed bat. *AP/WWP*

SIX WINS, NO LOSSES, ONE MEETING

Team meetings usually follow losses, generally a bunch of losses. However, in 1981 we had our first team meeting of the year before we even lost a game. It was called by Reggie Smith and Steve Garvey when we arrived in San Diego, where we went 2-7 a year earlier.

Long before I ever arrived, the Dodgers had been notorious for their flat play in San Diego. Many in the organization felt there were several contributing factors. One suggestion was that the proximity to home encouraged, let's say, conjugal visits, providing a distraction from the task at hand. Combine that with the underdog syndrome embraced by the Padres and their fans, which relished the chance to knock off what they perceived to be smug neighbors to the north.

Whatever the reason, the numbers proved that we would have won the division if we had just played decently there in 1980. So, the meeting was held and, although we played well that first night, the curse remained intact and we lost the series opener in 10 innings, 3-2. But with young catcher Mike Scioscia slugging a home run, Valenzuela put us right back on track the next night in another five-hit shutout, needing only 103 pitches for a 2-0 win, striking out 10 without a walk and singling twice. And he did it on three days' rest.

"I'm catching hell for not bringing him up sooner," Campanis said that night.

It was clear that the 20-year-old Valenzuela and Scioscia, the 22-year-old catcher, were clicking.

"Fernando and my career kind of paralleled each other," says Scisocia. "We were both young, and we both knew we had to figure it out or leave. We broke in together, we were pitcher and catcher and our senses of humor meshed."

In the series finale, Welch looked healthy, going six strong innings, and Ken Landreaux and Pedro Guerrero both homered in a 6-1 win over the Padres. That sent us to Houston with an 8-1 record, a 1.66 team ERA, and a three-game lead in the division. We dropped Houston again in the Astrodome opener, 5-2, raising our record to 9-1 and leaving the Astros in last place, already seven games back. Goltz, working out of the pen because by now we had so many healthy pitchers he couldn't get back into the rotation, picked up the save. We finally lost for the second time in our 11th game when Bob Knepper stopped us with a three-hitter, barely enough to beat Reuss, 1-0. We had now lost twice, both times by one run.

GUESS WHO'S THE STOPPER?

We could have lost again the following night, but Valenzuela wouldn't allow it. He drove in our only run with one of his two singles, pitched his fourth complete-game victory and third shutout, and struck out 11 batters. Returning to Dodger Stadium, Sutcliffe and Howe combined again to beat the Padres on April 23, 3-1, improving the team's mark to 11-2 and lowering the team ERA to 1.47.

We finally played a bad game the next night, blowing a 4-1 lead. We wasted two homers from Garvey and one from Davey Lopes, six strong innings from Welch, and finally lost, albeit by one run again, 6-5. But we avoided our first losing streak of the year the next night when I tripled home Ron Cey in the 11th inning for a 2-1 win. We started another win streak the next night when Smith doubled in Garvey from second base to give Reuss a 3-2 win over San Diego.

Valenzuela was proving to be nearly as accomplished a hitter as a pitcher, which he showed by going 3-for-4 against the Giants on April 27 in a 5-0 shutout win. That made the line for Fernando: five starts, five complete games, four shutouts, 45 innings, one earned run, an ERA of 0.20 (0.14 lifetime). More importantly for the team, our third win in a row raised our record to 14-3 and our lead in the division to four and a half games. Although we dropped a pair of games at the end of the month, we finished April with a 14-5 mark and a three-game lead over Cincinnati.

May started with our first trip of the year East, beginning with a split of a four-game series against the Expos in Montreal. Cey won one game with a home run that tied him with Carl Furillo for fourth on the all-time franchise home run list. Smith's RBI pinch-single in the 10th broke a 1-1 tie in the third game and we went on to present Fernando with his sixth victory without a loss.

Steve Garvey battled through injury in the first half of the season, but he was the Dodgers' answer to Mr. October, hitting .359 over the three postseason series.

FERNANDO ON BROADWAY

After winning two of three in Philadelphia, we bussed into New York and turned Fernando loose on the Big Apple. He didn't just take a bite out of it, he swallowed it whole. This was no masterpiece, as Freddy needed 142 pitches, walked five hitters, and the Mets stranded 10 base runners. But he bobbed and weaved his way to a seven-hit shutout, raising his record to 7-0 with five shutouts and lowering his ERA to a microscopic 0.29.

"I have to be careful on defense," said Baker at the time. "Sometimes I get to watching him too much."

This game, however, also gave a glimpse of what would become Valenzuela's greatest strength on the mound: the ability to escape jams and get outs even without his best stuff. Accepting challenges seemed to fit Fernando's personality.

"He was shy and introverted and very difficult to get into, but when he met with the media, he never refused to answer a question, no matter how many times it was asked before," recalls Jarrin. "He was a man of few words then, but very strong and very honest.

"If he was asked to do something, an autograph or an interview, he often would say no at first, then 10 seconds later he would do it. It was part of his sense of humor. He was well-liked by his teammates, and some of them tried to protect him that first year. Welch became one of his closest friends that year."

By the time we returned to Los Angeles, we led the division by 4½ games once again.

"I've never had a team get off to such a fast start with so little," said Lasorda at the time. "It's been the pitching."

FERNANDO HAD SOME HELP

When hasn't it been the pitching for the Dodgers?

"You could count on our four starters that year to go out there on their regular day," says Reuss, who was one of them. "You could count on them pretty much like clockwork. And, in any day and age, that's rare to find. But it was the right combination of pitchers; we had good balance with two right-handers and two-lefthanders and it was also four different looks.

"You had Bobby Welch, who was a hard-throwing righthander with a dominating curveball. Burt Hooton, his third-best pitch was his fastball; his best pitch was his changeup. But he could throw his knuckle-curveball and his changeup for a strike whenever he wanted, so his command to both sides of the plate was probably as good as anyone, and this was the prime of his career.

"And myself, with a newfound cutter, I went from a high-ball pitcher, a high-strikeout, high-walk kind of pitcher to more of a ground-ball, control-type pitcher and I was able to get through games with a lot fewer pitches and register a lot more complete games. Because of the number of ground balls that I threw, the infield played a lot better behind me, I think, than they did the other guys because I got a lot of early-count outs and because they were anticipating a lot of ground balls. So they played above average for me.

"And when you put it all together, and then you add Fernando, and you've got a look that no one else had in the league. Fernando, at an early age, had pitching savvy beyond his years. And with Mike Scioscia behind the plate, you saw things with the baseball that I never thought were possible. Changeups, fastballs inside, and Fernando being able to make up pitches to locations at a young age, it was probably the equivalent of watching a genius paint or a prodigy play piano.

"At 20, Fernando was getting the complete games, he was getting the attention, and that was pretty good, because the rest of us were able to go about our business under the radar. And the four of us put together some pretty good numbers as far as ERA and wins. Our pitching success allowed the offense and defense to catch up and put some runs on the board, and it was a deadly combination."

Reuss also revealed that the Dodger reputation for pitching was by plan, not accident.

"During spring training the first season I was with the club, in '79, Don Sutton pulled me aside [like I guess guys before him did] and took it upon himself to give me a lay of the land and tell me that it's going be different here than I've ever had it or will ever have it anywhere else," Reuss remembers.

"And I didn't know what the hell he was talking about, but he said, 'We do our own training here.' And he went on to explain how they did aerobic work, which is jogging and running distance, and then on alternate days they do the anaerobic work, the sprints and that sort of thing. The pitching coach doesn't control that unless you want him to,

Burt Hooton might have been lost in the shuffle, but he was probably the best pitcher in baseball (not named Fernando Valenzuela) during the first half of the 1981 season.

but all of the starters had opted to run that way, and this had begun before Sutton got there. It began with Sandy Koufax and Don Drysdale and was carried on through Claude Osteen, Bill Singer, Tommy John, and eventually it got to Sutton.

"And Sutton said, 'This is the way we do it. And if you're not on this program, you better get onto this program, because we're not going to have somebody come along here and drag us down and bring us back to where everybody else is. We feel that this is an advantage, this program, and it gives us a certain amount of freedom, so we want to keep it this way.' And that spring, I got onto the program, along with the Nautilus program, which is actually the first offseason that I did any kind of weights. You put that together, the distance program and the cut fastball and it remade me at close to 30 years old."

CEY HEY

Although our pitching was getting most of the attention, our offense picked up in May, as we reeled off another seven-game win streak. Cey had always been a fast starter, and he was really rolling by the middle of the month. He homered twice in a May 12 shutout over Montreal, and his tie-breaking homer (sixth in nine games) the next night beat the Expos again.

The following night, Cey went 0-for-4, but nobody noticed because Fernando went to 8-0, matching Boo Ferris of the 1945 Boston Red Sox for winning his first eight Major League starts. And it wasn't easy. He gave up a solo home run for the first time in his Major League career to Chris Speier in the third inning, marking the first time that the Dodgers had trailed all year in a game started by Valenzuela. Garvey's two-run bloop single gave us a 2-1 lead that Valenzuela took into the ninth, but he served up a solo home run to Andre Dawson in the top of the ninth that tied the game. Guerrero led off the bottom of the ninth with a walk-off homer off Steve Ratzer, Guerrero's sixth of the year.

That extended our division lead to 5½ games, but our hot streak wasn't over. We closed out the homestand with a three-game sweep of the Mets. Cey won the first game with a bases-loaded, tie-breaking single in the ninth after Guerrero's game-tying homer. Cey then drove in three runs in a 9-0 shutout by Hooton in the second game, and followed that with a homer in a 6-1 series finale win.

The Penguin now had eight homers and 19 RBI, after ending April with no homers and two RBI. But more importantly, we had a seven-game win streak and the best record in baseball at 26-9.

FREDDY'S HUMAN, AND SO'S OUR TEAM

All good things must end as they say, and in this case it was time for Valenzuela's streak—as well as our team's streak—to come to a close. The defending-champion Phillies shut us out, 4-0, on May 18, scoring three runs off Valenzuela in the same inning. We had started to wonder if something like that was even possible. He had allowed only four runs in 72 innings all year. And he allowed only three hits in seven innings, but it resulted in a loss in front of, among others, Fernando's parents, who were watching him pitch in the big leagues for the first time.

We lost another one-run game to the Phillies the following night, then won one on my 10th-inning pinch-hit homer off lefthander Tug McGraw to prevent getting swept. I carried the bat halfway down the first-base line on my walk-off homer and told the writers afterward I didn't want to miss any of it while putting down the bat.

By May 23, we had raced out to a 29-11 record and a 6½-game lead over Cincinnati. Fernando's hot start overshadowed the fact that Hooton went 6-0 and Jerry Reuss was 4-1.

"That's nice for me," said Hooton. "It kind of lets me slip in the backdoor."

So, all of the pieces were falling into place in this season of urgency. We had the able veterans and the sensational rookie. We got off to a phenomenal start—but we would soon realize just how critical that fast start would be.

"No way somebody's going to finish ahead of us," predicted Guerrero.

Overshadowed somewhat by the success of our starting pitchers and the clutch hitting of our regulars was the difficulty Lasorda was having finding a righthanded complement to our lefthanded closer, Steve Howe. After the demise of Stanhouse, Lasorda tried Bobby Castillo and Goltz. But it was Dave Stewart who came through in Cincinnati during the final week of May. The rookie helped us beat the Reds in 12 innings, 4-2. We split the four-game series, winning Fernando's start in 10 innings, and left Ohio with a 6½-game lead.

As the season progressed, opposing teams began to adjust to Valenzuela. Scouting reports were undoubtedly telling hitters to lay off of Fernando's screwball, especially with a majority of those screwballs being thrown out of the strike zone. In spite of a couple of rocky starts, Fernando's ERA was still just an eye-popping 1.24 as May was drawing to an end!

As teammates, we got to see Fernando behind the scenes. From my vantage point, I believe the waves of media asking the same questions over and over started to get to him. He was too nice a kid and he was trying to accommodate too many people, which seemed to be taking a toll.

For all the attention given Freddy, Burt Hooton was having a season nearly as sensational. When we won the opener of a series in Atlanta on May 25, with Garvey slugging a home run and driving in three, it raised Happy's record to 7-0 and lowered his ERA to 1.96. It was a tribute to all of the hard work Hooton had done during the off-season, when Dr. Frank Jobe discovered weakness in Hooton's throwing shoulder and prescribed a strengthening program that has since become routine for most pitchers.

"I feel like a kid with something new to play with, something I haven't had for a year and a half," Hooton said at the time.

We were rained out in Atlanta on Tuesday night, but the real ominous clouds were up the East Coast in New York, where negotiations with the owners and the Players Association were going nowhere. The two sides had to reach an agreement by Friday of that week, or the players were ready to strike. We lost our next two games in Atlanta. Fernando was beaten by 42-year-old Gaylord Perry and, for the first time, left the clubhouse without speaking to the media. Meanwhile, the labor negotiators agreed on a week's reprieve until June 8, and the team headed home, our division lead now at 4½ games.

What would be our final homestand before the strike started with Pedro Guerrero driving in four runs in a 5-2 win over Cincinnati. The Reds then blemished Hooton's flashy start with a 9-1 whipping, our third loss in four games. We committed three errors and played sloppy ball every inning. A couple of the players went to Lasorda in the eighth or ninth inning to tell him we wanted to hold a players-only meeting immediately following the game to get our focus back on track. It was an even worse game than what the numbers showed. We stunk up the place.

Tommy told us that he was going to "chew some fannies" with his own meeting, but if there was still something left to talk about after that, we had the go-ahead. After Tommy's meeting, the players held one, too—and neither one of them was "G-Rated." But those meetings helped us get righted as a team and move on from the horrible game we had just lost.

In the rubber game the next day, it looked like we'd end the month with more of the same. We spotted Cincinnati a 4-0 lead and Reuss left in the first inning with a hamstring strain. But our offense caught fire in a seven-run third inning, and we added six more runs in the seventh. Our pitching staff held its ground, and when the dust settled we had a 16-4 win.

Dave Stewart was just a kid in 1981, but he stepped up to give Tommy Lasorda another option in the bullpen.

The victory only counted once, but it was a huge one for us. We needed to respond in a positive fashion to the embarrassment from the night before, and we needed to prove to ourselves that we were back as a team. Mission accomplished.

June started with Fernando back in his groove for a 5-2 win over the Braves. I hit a two-run homer in the first inning, and Freddy never relinquished the lead. The writers asked me afterward if I had been worried about Fernando. I told them the only concern I had about Fernando was whether he would get to the park safely.

But Fernando's win was quickly pushed from our minds when the team regressed in embarrassing fashion. We lost back-to-back games to a pair of 42-year-olds, our second loss to Gaylord Perry in a matter of days, followed by a defeat at the hands of Phil Niekro. But what I remember the most from our 4-2 loss to Niekro and the Braves had nothing to do with the game. That day I read an article written by syndicated columnist Dave Anderson. It was about a robbery, and it stayed with me for a long time. Dave wrote about some of the former Dodgers who returned for a special event in Brooklyn, "but one of them wuz robbed." Carl Erskine, Russ Meyer, and Sandy Amoros of the 1955 World Series Champion Dodgers were among those attending the event.

Two men held up Meyer at gunpoint. They took his cash, his watch and, worse—much worse—his two World Series rings. The robbery itself took place in Manhattan, on the corner of Lexington Avenue and 25th street. Russ said his disappointment wasn't about the money, but there was just no way he could replace the two rings and all the memories and pride that they represented to him.

Back on the field, we weren't doing anything worth remembering. While the strike deadline was repeatedly delayed to allow for talks that seemingly accomplished nothing, we weren't accomplishing much more as a team. On June 6, Fernando was shelled by the Cubs, 11-5, and our losing streak reached four games while our lead in the division slipped to 2½ games. Valenzuela's ERA over his last five starts was 6.96.

Although he was pitching only every four games, it was no coincidence that when he started losing, so did we.

Bob Welch restored order with a six-hit shutout win over the Cubs, but it was clear our momentum had hit a wall when we arrived in St. Louis and the Cardinals handed Hooton his third consecutive loss in the opener of that series. Our lead over the Reds, once 6½ games, was now down to just 1½ games.

Meanwhile, a judge rejected a request by the National Labor Relations Board for an injunction against the owners, and Marvin Miller responded with a memorandum to all players that the strike would begin before games on June 12, just three days away.

MAGIC NUMBER IN JUNE?

On Wednesday, June 10, with a Friday strike set, we found ourselves in something of a stretch drive earlier than anticipated. We had a 1½-game lead with—possibly—only two games left in the regular season. We had no idea how long the strike would last, so we had to consider this June series with the Cardinals our stretch drive.

If our magic number really was one, Jerry Reuss, our player rep, essentially clinched it for us that night, retiring 22 consecutive batters at one point and allowing just three hits in a complete-game 4-1 win over the Cardinals. Reuss, whose record now stood at 5-2, emphasized once again that the Dodgers pitching staff as a whole was flying way under baseball's radar screen. While most eyes were fixed on "Fernandomania," we never lost sight of the fact we had a damn good pitching *staff*.

Despite the key win, there was no champagne or celebration in the clubhouse afterward. The atmosphere was too surreal, as the following night's game would prove. With the strike looming, Valenzuela pitched well enough to win in a game he lost, 2-1, leaving his record at 9-4 and his ERA at 2.45. The game was all the more remarkable when we realized that the reason for a large police presence was that our rookie was the target of a death threat.

This game also saw Reggie Smith pinch-hit for ironman Steve Garvey in the ninth inning with us trailing by a run. Tommy explained after the game that he was hoping for a tying home run, an indication that the sprained wrist nagging Garvey was hampering his power worse than we thought. Garvey later admitted so.

"The more I played with it, the weaker it got until I couldn't drive the ball," he recalls. "That last game, Tommy needed a home run and I told him I couldn't get it done. If it had gotten any worse, I would have had to sit out and the (consecutive games) streak would have ended. I dodged the bullet. You could say the strike benefited me, because about three weeks into the strike, my wrist was in good shape."

Nonetheless, we had just finished an unfinished season in first place, if only by one-half game.

5

PARDON THE INTERRUPTION

ernando did some amazing things that rookie season, but one thing he couldn't do was save baseball from itself. On May 29, the executive board of the Players Association had unanimously voted to strike if the negotiations failed to settle the compensation issue. The deadline had been extended briefly after the Players Association's unfair labor complaint was heard by the National Labor Relations Board. But on June 12, Marvin Miller, executive director of the Major League Baseball Players Association, declared "The strike is on," announcing the first in-season walkout in baseball history.

At issue was free-agent compensation. Owners losing a free-agent player wanted to receive a "ranking" player as compensation for every player they lost. Players (actually, the union) objected, arguing that such a system would restrict movement. From the previous Collective Bargaining Agreement, clubs received amateur draft picks as compensation when a free agent signed elsewhere.

In 1980, players held an eight-day walkout in spring training. In 1972, players struck for the first 13 days of the season, but nobody was really prepared for a work stoppage during the season, and it was unthinkable that it would go on for 50 days.

Every Major League player was aware of continuing labor differences between the teams' ownership and the Players Association and the very strong possibility of a work stoppage. But June 12 was still a gigantic and gut-wrenching shock. That was the day, with the authority of the executive board of the Players Association, Marvin Miller decided to strike as the owners continued to demand the erosion of what we had previously won through bargaining. We were just "players," not businessmen, but even we knew that you can't just arbitrarily take back what you bargained away. So we took a stand.

STRANDED IN ST. LOUIE

We were in St. Louis when the players went on strike, and Reuss, our rep, was keeping us up to date on the progress. The team was left in limbo, as the entire situation was confusing to say the least. Some of us wondered if the strike was going to last just overnight. Should everybody stay put and not leave? If we were to leave for L.A., would it be on our own dime? The Dodgers owned their airplane, a Boeing 720B named the Kay-O II (after Kay O'Malley, wife of owner Walter O'Malley).

We finally got word that the players would be taken to the airport on the team busses, but we were not allowed to fly home on the Dodgers plane. We were on our own. Most of our younger players were in a panic. Some didn't have enough money to purchase a plane ticket back home. Others didn't know if they should go back to L.A. or fly to their actual homes in other states and just sit by the telephone. It was a mess. To top it off, the team plane was parked right outside the big window of the terminal, and we watched all eight front-office employees walk onboard for their flight home.

Forty-five minutes later, the Dodgers plane was still parked. We got word there was some sort of engine trouble onboard the Kay-O II, and Capt. Lew Carlisle told everyone it would take a couple of hours to repair. Off came some of the eight who had boarded an hour earlier, including Al Campanis.

I think Al was trying to make the best of the already-bad situation when he asked some of the players if he could join them as they were getting something to eat. There was a mixed array of feelings at that moment. Some were angered at not being able to fly back home on the almost-empty Dodgers plane, while others were just too busy trying to make their own travel plans and help others. Al's hands were tied by Major League Baseball at that point, but to his credit he tried to soothe some frayed nerves, although most had already snapped.

When Capt. Lew finally took off with his load of eight, the feeling of emptiness set in for those of us still staring out the terminal window. The dreams we had shared since our childhood of playing Major League Baseball were put on hold as the Dodgers plane disappeared on the horizon.

SOLIDARITY SAVED US

One thing we knew going into this thing was that the players needed to stay in touch with each other. We didn't have the public relations outlets that the Major League Baseball clubs did, and the need to hear what was really going on during negotiations was paramount. We needed to get straight answers and not comment on something we knew little about.

"They told us it was going to be over in a week," recalls Dusty Baker. "And I remember loaning Dave Stewart and Rudy Law some money to get home because they wouldn't take us home on the Dodger plane because it was a strike. So we had to pay our own way home. And so we started working out at the University of Southern California and, somehow, when we showed up, balls and bats mysteriously showed up, even though none of us brought them."

There was nothing mysterious about it if you knew that Tommy Lasorda's good friend, the late Rod Dedeaux, was the legendary Trojan baseball coach.

"We made sure that stuff was there," says Lasorda. "I wanted those guys ready to play when it was over."

I reminded Dusty that the intensity of our workouts sort of lagged as the strike dragged on.

"At first, everybody was there," recalls Baker. "And as the strike went longer and longer and longer, fewer and fewer guys worked out. And I remember, half the team lived in the Valley, and the other half of the team lived down in Orange County. And so I remember working out a lot with Lee Lacy, because he lived near me. We'd be doing something every day, and it got to be drudgery doing baseball every day. So I started swimming, doing different things to stay in shape because I just knew, in my mind and my heart, that the strike wasn't going to go the whole season. I didn't have any clue in '94 that it was going to take the rest of the season. But in '81 I knew we'd come back.

"And I remember in '81 when I made the All-Star team—I guess based on what I'd done the first half—I was so glad I worked out as hard as I did, because, I'm not bragging, but I think that year I had the highest batting average in the league after the strike."

The strike was tough on everybody, but especially the young players who hadn't earned enough money to get through the hiatus without a paycheck. Some of them had to find work, like Dave Stewart, who got a job at a hardware firm. Others did autograph signings at local malls.

On July 29, Marvin Miller held the first of what was scheduled to be two to three regional meetings with players around the country to update everyone on where the negotiations stood. The first meeting was held in Los Angeles. About 50 players attended, and before the meeting was over, we had voted unanimously to support the stance Marvin had taken. The support came in a voice vote, suggested by Rod Carew of the California Angels, following the 2½-hour meeting.

Our Dodger player rep, Jerry Reuss, summed up the meeting by commenting: "If someone had an objection, damn it, they could say something."

The next meeting was to take place in New York the following day, but it never happened. After weeks of workouts and what appeared to be wasted days and nights failing to reach a settlement, the phone finally rang with good news—the strike had been settled and the season was to resume in about two weeks. The owners had thoughtfully taken out $50 million in strike insurance, and their insurance payments had finally run out. So they called for an end to the clamor and decided to give in to the union's demands.

A SETTLEMENT WITHOUT PEACE

On July 30, a marathon negotiating session resulted in a compromise. In the settlement, teams that lost a "premium" free agent could be compensated by drawing from a pool of players left unprotected from all of the clubs rather than just the signing team. The settlement gave the owners what I considered a "limited victory" on the compensation issue.

The players, for the most part, won their point. But at what cost? The fifth work stoppage in Major League Baseball history lasted seven weeks and one day, and forced the cancellation of 713 games (or 38 percent of the regular season). An estimated $146 million was lost in player salaries, ticket sales, broadcast revenues, and concessions. The players lost $4 million a week in salaries, while the owners suffered a total loss of $72 million.

And everybody was mad. On June 27, the Associated Press reported that Dodgers management claimed three players had violated their contracts during the strike. Al Campanis, the Dodgers general manager, claimed in a statement that Fernando Valenzuela, Pedro Guerrero, and Pepe Frias had played in exhibition games in Mexico over the weekend, something prohibited by their contracts. Campanis said: "Their participation is a violation of the uniform players contract, and we are gathering information on the details of what took place. We will determine appropriate action once we have all the necessary information."

When Fernando was contacted in Mexico City, the rookie pitching star acknowledged he had played in Tijuana, but denied he had accepted any payment for playing. Fernando had a great line for the media, simply saying: "I don't collect for exhibitions."

This was only the tip of the iceberg, however. The players were still mad about being forced to go on strike to protect what we had already negotiated. The owners were mad because they tried to force our hand and lost, and they weren't happy with the legal advice for which they had paid dearly. And the fans were really mad. They were angry with the players, the owners, the game of baseball, and the people in charge! I felt very strongly that every one of us in baseball better bury the hatchet and get on with promoting our game. Our great game of Major League Baseball hadn't been great at all for seven weeks and one hell of a long day.

There were more questions than answers on myriad topics connected with the just-ended strike, including the burning question: "Did we do the right thing and did we *all* learn anything to help protect the future of our great game?" While most people tried to figure out exactly who was to blame for the work stoppage, an important piece of business was finally decided upon: The season was still salvageable, even though we had lost what represented one-third of the schedule to the strike.

SPLITSVILLE

The final decision to change how the remainder of the season would be played, announced August 6, brought on almost as much confusion as the strike itself. The split-season formula won approval in a vote of the club owners, who declared the four teams leading their respective divisions when the strike commenced—Los Angeles, Philadelphia, Oakland, and the Yankees—the winners of the "first half." These winners would play a best-of-five game series against the "second half" winners. If the same team won both halves, the team with the second-best overall record would advance.

That last part was changed August 20 to protect the "integrity" of the game, according to commissioner Bowie Kuhn, who had come under fire for the arrangement after managers Tony La Russa of the White Sox and Whitey Herzog of the Cardinals said they would intentionally have their clubs lose games if it meant helping their playoff chances. So Kuhn decided that if one club finished first in both half-seasons, it would play the team that finished second in the second half. It was the first time that Major League Baseball had used a split-season format since 1892, and it was obvious with all the controversy to see why it had been suppressed for so long.

The split-season format, although it would allow each league to recoup some revenue lost during the strike by adding an extra round of playoffs, was not without its flaws. All of the first-half winners lacked the same motivation to keep winning and had to struggle with the desire to just cruise through the second half. Even worse, Cincinnati (NL West) and St. Louis (NL East) each failed to make the playoffs, despite finishing 1981 with the best combined full-season records in their divisions. Those teams were some kind of bitter about the way they were excluded. Our divisional rivals were outraged. The Reds had won their last seven games of the first half to finish one-half game behind us. But they had also played one fewer game than we had, so in their minds, the playing field wasn't even.

"I remember how incensed the Reds were," recalls Peter O'Malley. "I still stay in touch with (former Reds general manager) Bob Howsam, and he often talks about it. We haven't talked about it in a few years, but he was outraged."

In contrast to the Reds' and Cardinals' bad luck, Kansas City made the postseason despite having the fourth-best full-season record in their seven-team division. The Royals finished in fifth during the first half with a 20-30 record, but made the best of their fresh start in the second half by winning the division with a 30-23 record.

SPRING TRAINING IN SUMMER

With the strike over, teams had just a couple of weeks to get ready for Opening Day, take two. It wasn't impossible for players who had continued to work out diligently throughout the strike. But who were we kidding? Having a leisurely workout with some buddies maybe two or three days a week is light years away from working out every day in earnest. Unfortunately, most of us didn't take our workouts too seriously. The only way to get our team 100 percent ready to play again was to do it the right way, and it was going to hurt for a few days!

Players showed up on July 31 for workouts at Dodger Stadium. Some, like Davey Lopes, were wearing beards that had been banned by club policy. Valenzuela appeared to have dropped a few pounds, and the rest of us were hopeful the time off did his arm some good, because after his first eight wins, his ERA the remainder of the first half was 6.46. At that first workout, Tommy decided to throw batting practice.

"He probably put us all in slumps, knowing Tommy," jokes Yeager. "With that, we were probably hitting more off ourselves than hitting off Lasorda with that hanging curveball that he threw. It had more hang-time than a Ray Guy punt, you know?

"But that was Tommy. He worked with all of us religiously and Tommy thought if he got out on the mound and we had some game situations then we would get back in shape. I don't remember too much, but I know we were there just laughing and carrying on and trying to hit that hanging curveball."

Yeager wasn't laughing at the end of one particular workout, however. It was late in the afternoon, shadows had darkened the entire infield, and Yeager, taking batting practice off reliever Steve Howe, drilled the pitcher in the forehead with a line drive.

"I thought he was dead, man," said Dave Stewart.

Howe couldn't see for a few hours and was woozy, but luckily escaped serious injury and was ready to go for the second half. And we sure needed him.

We were all a little curious about how the fans would react, and we got our first taste on August 6, when we played an exhibition game against our Triple-A affiliate Albuquerque at Dodger Stadium. The crowd was big, an estimated 45,000. There were cheers, but there were also a lot of boos from a hometown crowd that almost never booed its Dodgers.

THE ALL-STAR GAME

Six Dodgers were selected to appear in the August 9 All-Star Game: Lopes, Baker, Guerrero, Valenzuela, Burt Hooton, and Steve Garvey. And none of them knew what to expect for the game. How would the fans react, was it going to get ugly, would there be protests, would the players that night be typecast as the villains? We didn't know, but we all watched the game just to see what took place.

What we saw, thank goodness, was a baseball game, nine innings of competition to whet the appetite of every baseball player and fan around the country who tuned in. A record crowd of 72,086 turned out for a night of fireworks, as the Nationals pounded four home runs en route to a 10th-straight victory over the American League, 5-4. A record number of 56 players saw action in the game.

Baseball was back! Thank *god!* The game that night was a terrific way to start the second half of a disrupted season.

6

BACK TO WORK

Some people were still angry with those of us in "the game," but it was back to business in the baseball world after the All-Star game. What I missed during that long layoff—and still do to this very day—was the competition and pure excitement of Major League Baseball. I missed the camaraderie of a group of individuals coming together as a united team trying to actually live out our dreams: to play Major League Baseball and play it well enough to get to the "Fall Classic," the World Series.

There's no way around the fact that the urgency with which we started the 1981 season had diminished after the strike. We knew that no matter how we played during the second half, we were in the playoffs.

"During the second half I really took on a completely different mindset," says Cey. "I was kind of treading water, because we only had, what, 50 games left? We had already been guaranteed a playoff spot and I didn't have quite the same impetus or attitude, because what I was thinking about was, let's just fine-tune this thing until we get to the postseason. Everything's in place, and all these other teams are out there battling for this other spot."

RE-OPENING DAY

The second Opening Day of 1981 was accompanied by a television blackout of most games across the country. Monday night was reserved for ABC's nationally televised game, and the network's contract with Major League Baseball required exclusivity, so no other games could be televised in competition with the ABC game. Everyone across the nation with hopes of watching the return of baseball was going to see the Cincinnati Reds versus the Los Angeles Dodgers, or St. Louis Cardinals versus the Philadelphia Phillies. The primary game was our matchup with the Reds, with the network planning to break away periodically for updates on the effort of Pete Rose to break Stan Musial's National League record for career hits.

The Reds, of course, were seething over the settlement that wasted their surge in the final days before the strike. Jerry Reuss and Steve Howe combined to shut them out in the first game back. But Fernando followed by getting knocked out in the fourth inning the next night, and we went on to lose another close one, 7-6.

General manager Al Campanis, who spent some of the strike downtime scouting our minor league affiliates, called up relievers Tom Niedenfuer and Alejandro Peña and second baseman Steve Sax. They replaced Rick Sutcliffe and Davey Lopes (who were injured), and Joe Ferguson (who was released). Sax's arrival was particularly telling, because it reinforced the notion that Lopes's days with the club were numbered, and our time as a unit—split season or not—was running out.

REGGIE VERSUS THE PIRATES

Toward the end of August, we swept the Pirates in a three-game series in Pittsburgh, but one of those games was marred by a memorable confrontation involving Reggie Smith and almost the entire Pittsburgh team. On August 25, I had a pinch-hit single in the 11th inning that broke a tie, and I scored when Bill Russell followed with a hit. But the headlines didn't focus on the heroics on the field; instead they blared about the near-riot under the stands.

According to Mark Heisler's account in the *Los Angeles Times*, Pirates pitcher Pascual Perez set the stage in the sixth inning when he hit Dusty Baker with a pitch after just missing Baker on the previous pitch. Perez also had hit Bill Russell a few batters earlier and had almost hit Baker in the first inning. Catcher Tony Peña assured Baker that Perez was not intentionally throwing at us, but Reggie was having none of that, and he was all over Perez, shouting at him from our dugout.

Although Reggie was 40 pounds heavier than Perez, the Pirates pitcher started yelling back from the mound. When the inning ended, Perez pointed toward the dugout, clearly suggesting that Reggie meet him to settle their differences out of sight. Perez then ran toward the hallway off the Pirate dugout that led to a narrow walkway under the stands that connected the two clubhouses. When Perez took off into his dugout, Reggie did the same through ours. Teammates followed, and the field suddenly was drained of participants, with only umpires remaining. Writers raced down from the press box, only to find the hallway jammed. And all of this while a game was supposedly being played.

Pirates manager Chuck Tanner was yelling at security guards to get the media out of the area, as if they were the problem. The writers asked me how close the teams got to each other.

"Pretty well to the Mason-Dixon line," I said. "Let's put it this way, air traffic controllers don't let jets get that close."

A high level of intensity can turn a good player into an exceptional one. Reggie Smith led the league in intensity every year he played. *MLB Photos via Getty Images*

Valenzuela appeared to return to form with a shutout of the Cubs on August 27, and about the same time we seemed to return to form, winning five straight, moving us into first place for the first time in the second half. But it didn't last long. We ended the month with a three-game losing streak, and in one of the games I was ejected for asking home plate umpire Bruce Froemming about a strike call.

HEARING FOOTSTEPS

That was just the normal day-to-day flare-up, but the tensions created by the "kids" were another matter. With Lopes nursing injuries, the energetic Sax got enough playing time to indicate what was to come. Davey didn't appreciate sharing time with Sax when he returned and said so to the media. The September call-up of Mike Marshall, who won the triple crown at Triple-A Albuquerque, was a sign that Steve Garvey wouldn't be playing first base in Los Angeles forever, either. And Candy Maldonado had his eye on Reggie Smith's spot in the outfield.

Making the best of the situation, the veterans seized a money-making opportunity during early batting practice one day. After taking $20 apiece in the first meeting, the Old Goats suckered the Young Studs into a rematch at $50 each, and we won that one, too. "Like taking candy from a baby," I told the writers.

To be fair, the 1981 season wouldn't have been so memorable without the contributions of the "older" younger players, like Scioscia and Guerrero. Although they lacked the bitter taste of postseason defeat, they played like veterans.

According to Scioscia, they had no choice.

"Everybody knew their role and there was no fooling around," Scioscia recalls. "This team was extremely accountable. The veterans were hardcore. There was no orientation for a young player. You did your job or you were out of there. The veterans' favorite line to one of the young guys when he'd do something wrong was, 'You're messing

Injuries to Davey Lopes provided playing time in 1981 for rookie Steve Sax, who turned that into the start of an All-Star career.

with my playoff money. What's wrong with you? Get your head out of your butt.'

"Guys like me, Pete, Saxy, and Marshall—we were told in no uncertain terms what was expected of us to win. There was no time for developing your skills. You did the job.

"But that was the trademark of the organization back then. Along with the veteran stars, there was always a group of talented young guys coming up, and the best ones survived. It was that way back to the Brooklyn days. The baton was passed to us and we passed the baton to the guys who followed. It wasn't an easy way to break in, but I wouldn't trade it. It was the most talented team I ever played on."

A BAD BREAK

Our biggest loss of the second half came on September 9, when Giants pitcher Tom Griffin broke Cey's left forearm with a fastball. Cey was lucky the pitch broke his arm, because it could have broken his face. He took one step away from home plate and slammed his batting helmet to the ground. Players know instantly if an injury is really bad, and Ron knew it right then.

A few hours later, the doctors told him they had rarely heard of a forearm being broken on the opposite side of the point of impact, but that is what happened. Ron was told he would be in a cast for five weeks, so he would miss the rest of the season. The doctors know medicine, but they didn't know Ron. He had his own timetable for returning.

We split the next eight games after Cey's injury. The last of those wins was a shutout of Atlanta by Fernando Valenzuela, who had become dominant at home playing in front of crowds that swelled thanks to a huge Latino turnout. Fernando had rediscovered whatever magic he had lost earlier in the season. When he shut out the Braves with a three-hitter, it was his fourth consecutive win and raised his record to 13-4. He had allowed only five runs over his last 50 innings and had lowered his season ERA to 2.36 after it had ballooned to a season-high 2.87 a month earlier.

But we dropped the next five games, including a sweep by Cincinnati, and a deficit of two games on September 18 had quickly grown to five games by September 23 as we sank to fourth place in the division. Our losing streak was snapped on September 24 in Candlestick Park, but it took all hell breaking loose to do it.

REGGIE VERSUS CANDLESTICK

How can I be diplomatic about describing Candlestick Park? Simply, it was a *dump*! The stadium featured a poor layout, miserable weather, and as always, "bad blood," when the Dodgers and Giants got together. Even before the Juan Marichal-John Roseboro incident in the '60s—when the Giants pitcher clubbed the Dodgers catcher on the head with his bat during an intense game that progressed into a violent brawl—the Dodger-Giant rivalry was a heated one. But on September 24, 1981, it got out of hand, and it included the fans, one in particular.

The Giants normally provided extra security when the Dodgers played at Candlestick, with at least one uniformed San Francisco Police Department officer stationed in the dugout. Over the years those officers have normally been the same ones on every trip north. They know us and we know them, and they do a great job.

On this night, one fan who appeared to have had too much to drink kept coming down to the far end of our dugout and yelling at the players, the batboy, the trainers—anyone associated with the Dodgers. There was nothing unusual about that as we were in enemy territory; they don't like us and we don't like them. But this particular guy kept yelling and drinking, and his language became more and more profane.

In the top of the sixth inning, it happened. Reggie Smith was walking back to the dugout from home plate when the guy came down again and *really* unloaded on Reggie with a barrage of profanity that would make a San Francisco longshoreman blush. Then the guy threatened to throw a Giant helmet he was wearing at Reggie.

I remember the calmness that Reggie showed in just looking up at the guy, who was continuing his verbal onslaught, and saying to him: "You can't be that stupid." That's when all hell broke loose. The idiot actually reared back and with all his might tried to take off Reggie's head with the helmet. Here came the helmet, and there went Reggie over to the railing at the end of the dugout, along with everybody else in a Dodger uniform!

This guy was nuts: He held his ground and continued swearing at everybody, saying he was going to "kick everybody's ass." For sure, there was an ass-kicking that took place that day, but it wasn't handed down by a San Francisco fan. Reggie jumped into the stands, while cops came down from the stands and out from the dugout and grabbed the guy. It was a mess. The guy was resisting the police as he held onto the metal railing that separates the stands from the playing field. The police told him repeatedly to let go of the railing and stop resisting arrest, but he didn't listen. He included the police in his tirade and said he would kick their asses, too!

The officers informed the idiot one final time to let go of the railing or they would be forced to use their billy clubs, and if they had to, break his fingers. He refused, and the officers were true to their word—out came the billy clubs. You could hear a couple of his fingers pop, and he finally let go of the rail and they dragged him away.

We won the game, by the way, 7-3, beating Tom Griffin, the pitcher whose fastball had broken Cey's arm. But despite the win, we were worried about what might happen to Reggie if he were disciplined by the league. On September 29, National League president Chub Feeney suspended Smith for five games and fined him $5,000 for going into the stands. The judgment seemed harsh to those of us who had witnessed the event up close and personal.

HUMBLED BY THE EXPRESS

We traveled to Houston, where Burt Hooton threw a complete-game shutout that looked pretty good until we saw what happened the next night. Nolan Ryan merely used us to make history, throwing a no-hitter, the fifth of his career, breaking a tie with former Dodger Sandy Koufax for the all-time record. It was hardly a nice way to prepare for the team we would face in the playoffs. The Astros went on to win the NL West in the second half, finishing 1 ½ games ahead of the Reds, who just missed the mark again.

The Astrodome was always a tough place to play, and for a couple of good reasons. First, the Astros always seemed to have pitchers who threw hard enough to knock down a brick wall. And second, it was always dark inside the dome, as if they had forgotten to flip some light switches.

We got only two hits the next day against former teammate Don Sutton in another loss to Houston, and one day later we were mathematically eliminated from the second-half "title" with a loss in Atlanta. Reduced to the role of spoiler the rest of the "regular" season, we wound up in fourth place for the second half, at 27-26.

Except for Cey's broken arm, we finished the season relatively healthy. The Astros, though, were left short-handed for the playoffs because a Reuss pitch had shattered Sutton's kneecap as he tried to bunt during a game on the final weekend of the season. But the Astros really had nothing to complain about, at least compared to the Reds, who were watching the playoffs from home.

7

WESTERN DIVISION PLAYOFFS

The Western Division playoff, a best-of-five series, opened in the Astrodome, where the Astros were determined to win the first two games because their 1-11 mark in Dodger Stadium during the 1981 season was an indication that they were in deep on the West Coast. We were still without Ron Cey, and the Astros were minus Don Sutton.

"I told the guys," Lasorda recalls, "that we were going to win with the Penguin or without him. I had to shake the guys up. We needed to have the fire in the belly and believe we could win."

A year earlier, we trailed the Astros by three games with a season-ending three-game series between the two of us in Los Angeles, which we dramatically swept to force a sudden-death, one-game playoff, only to lose that game and be eliminated.

GAME 1:
RYAN AGAIN

This series opened October 6 in what looked on paper to be a classic pitching duel between Fernando Valenzuela and Nolan Ryan, who just 10 days before had no-hit us. Fernando pitched brilliantly, allowing just one run across eight innings to match Ryan, who tossed a two-hitter but allowed a solo home run to Steve Garvey in the seventh inning.

Garvey's shot turned out to be our only run and tied the game at 1-1 heading into the bottom of the ninth. Leading off the top of the ninth, Valenzuela was lifted for a pinch-hitter. So Dave Stewart was called upon in the bottom of the frame. Stew recorded two quick outs, then Craig Reynolds hit a pinch-hit single and Alan Ashby slugged a two-out, two-run homer over the right-field fence to give the Astros a 3-1 victory. Houston was halfway to its initial goal of a sweep in the Astrodome.

GAME 2:
ANOTHER NAIL-BITER

Game 2 the following night was a lower scoring, if not a better pitched, duel. Jerry Reuss, a former Astro, gave us nine scoreless innings of five-hit ball, but we couldn't get the clutch hit against Houston starter Joe Niekro and stranded 10 runners in Niekro's eight innings of work. The Astros had runners at first and second with one out in the bottom of the ninth, but stranded both runners to send the scoreless game to extra innings.

In the 11th inning, the Astros bench again pulled off another minor miracle against Stewart. Phil Garner and Tony Scott singled to start the inning and chase Stewart. Terry Forster then retired Jose Cruz on a fly to left, and Tom Niedenfuer was called upon to seal the deal. He intentionally walked Cesar Cedeno to load the bases and then

Future major league managers Dusty Baker and Phil Garner react to an umpire's call during the 1981 Division Series.

struck out Art Howe for the second out. But Denny Walling's pinch-hit single to the right-center alley scored Garner, and the Astros had their two-games-to-none series lead.

DAY OFF:
WE'RE COOL

October 8 was an "off day" with no game. We were scheduled to have a team workout at Dodger Stadium, but the biggest hurdle that morning was avoiding the newspapers, radio, and television. Most commentators in the Los Angeles market were already 10 minutes into their Dodgers eulogy. Yes, we were down two games to none in a best-of-five series, but we weren't dead—yet! The sportswriters in the Los Angeles area are some of the best and fairest writers to deal with on a day-to-day basis, and many of them, I'm proud to say, are friends. But on this day the sports section looked more like the obit page to me.

When your back is against to the wall, it's interesting to see how people around you react. Do they run for the hills, just stand there and hope for the best, or get up, dust themselves off and give it their best shot? This group of Dodger players did the latter, without even taking the time to dust themselves off.

My drive to the stadium the following day was rather quiet—no radio surfing, at least not on the AM side, and no talk radio, especially sports. Today was a soft jazz FM day, but no call-in sports shows on AM radio. Traffic around the stadium wasn't packed, but there were a few cars and a couple of hand-made signs showing support for the Dodgers when I arrived.

Inside the locker room, the first thing I noticed were my sportswriter "friends" pawing at the carpeted floor, voices low, trying to see who might be willing to talk. They didn't have too much trouble with this group: We had some guys who were just goofy enough to say we had the Astros right where we wanted them. Come to think of it,

The entire team was leery of the media when we returned to Los Angeles down two games to none following Game 2 of the 1981 Division Series. Bill Russell would give the press its money's worth following Game 4, however, after singling home the game's decisive run.

we did—but we didn't know it at the time. We faced a heck of a steep climb, and none of us could afford to be out of step with the rest.

Robert Schweppe, now an aide to former club owner Peter O'Malley and then a front-office official, remembers the atmosphere in the clubhouse before Game 3 immediately after Tommy had given us a pep talk.

"I'm waiting outside the clubhouse," Schweppe recalls, "and the doors open. Tommy finishes [his speech], and Garvey stands up and says, 'Guys, just like Bill Murray said in *Meatballs*: It doesn't really matter. It doesn't really matter.' And the guys on the team started going with the chant, 'It doesn't really matter, it doesn't really matter.' And Garvey says, 'Oh, let's beat those mothers.' And I remember thinking, 'If nothing else, they're loose and they're not thinking, oh, we've gotta play a perfect game.'"

We knew the Astros, even needing only one win in three games, were not going to assume anything. After all, to conclude the previous season they were in the same boat and watched as three games vanished at Dodger Stadium. Each day they had come to the ballpark hoping for a celebration, waiting for somebody to pull it off, and each day they trudged back to the hotel without opening the champagne.

When the team was introduced along the third-base line during the pregame ceremonies, we couldn't help but notice the atmosphere was very different for the usually laid-back crowd at Dodger Stadium. Our fans were alive with energy and the place was rocking. Didn't they know the season was over if we didn't win three straight games? Maybe they had tuned out the media as well. The crowd didn't care about the deficit; they came out to support us and see a good baseball game. Sing the National Anthem and let's play ball!

GAME 3:
THE COMEBACK BEGINS

As if the crowd needed to get any more worked up, Cey was in uniform and he threw out the first pitch for Game 3. The crowd noise was deafening.

It wasn't Burt Hooton's turn in the rotation, but he got the ball from Lasorda instead of Bob Welch. Hooton responded by firing a three-hitter over seven innings, allowing just one run on a homer by Howe. We supported Happy with a three-run first inning that included a two-run homer from Garvey.

Looking back, that first inning was one of the biggest innings of the season for us. We were down 2-0 in the series, and we scored three runs in the first inning off Bob Knepper. I thought that was a huge momentum swing, especially with Hooton on the mound pitching his butt off.

Lasorda, playing the baseball manager, called on our stopper Steve Howe in the eighth inning. Howe pitched a perfect frame, striking out two batters. Then Tommy continued his gambling ways when he sent Reggie Smith to the plate to pinch-hit for Howe in the bottom of the eighth. Reggie hit a sacrifice fly to knock in our second of three runs that inning. Lasorda handed a 6-1 lead in the ninth to Welch, who closed out the win.

GAME 4:
FERNANDO HANGS TOUGH

The following day I faced another 33-mile drive from my home to Dodger Stadium. I had barely glanced at the headlines in the sports section of the newspaper that morning, but I could tell that the criticism had been toned down. However, we were still on the "critical list." So in the car I once again kept the radio tuned to strictly music stations.

"Fernandomania" was on tap for another must-win if we were to have another day of baseball in 1981. During my drive, I wondered which Fernando would be on the mound that night: the erratic one from a few starts ago, or the one who looked like he had dialed in his control over the last couple of games?

Dodgers fans were treated to the real deal. Fernando and Astros starter Vern Ruhle both took perfect games into the fifth inning. In the top of the fifth, Cesar Cedeno singled to get the Astros their first baserunner. But he was quickly erased when Fernando picked him off. Pedro Guerrero homered for us in the bottom of the fifth to score the game's first run. In the seventh, Bill Russell, playing with a stress fracture of his foot that would require offseason surgery, singled home Garvey with the decisive run. The Astros scored a run in the ninth, but Valenzuela hung on for a 2-1 victory. Fernando allowed just four hits in the game—two of them coming in the ninth—as we evened the series at two games apiece.

A raucous crowd of almost 56,000 roared in approval. The victory set up a fifth and deciding game, with both teams scheduled to have strong pitching on the mound. Reuss would face off against Ryan with the playoffs on the line.

"We all believed that coming home would be a big plus for us. To get even and then have the opportunity to win the damn thing at Dodger Stadium, that was a great deal of motivation for us to win the series," says Yeager.

GAME 5: REVENGE FOR 1980

The Game 5 duel unfolded as expected, with Ryan allowing just three baserunners through five scoreless innings. Watching Ryan warm up before the game, we could tell that his fastball and curve weren't in sync. The fact that he was still putting up zeroes on the scoreboard is a testament to his pitching prowess. But we were confident we'd get to him eventually—and we did.

Ryan showed a crack in the armor in the sixth when he walked Dusty Baker after Baker's foul pop-up fell untouched. We followed with a hit-and-run single by Garvey that moved Baker to third, and I singled him home. One out later, Scioscia singled in Garvey and I scored an unearned run when Russell knocked the ball out of first baseman Denny Walling's glove after his slow roller was fielded by third baseman Art Howe. Garvey tripled in another run in the seventh, and we won the division with a 4-0 shutout from Reuss, who allowed only five singles in the game.

We came close to overcoming the odds the previous October against this Houston club. This time, we won the Western Division in an unprecedented playoff against incredible odds and a terrific baseball team. I've witnessed some big games and some high emotions

Pedro Guerrero celebrates as he returns to the dugout after his fifth-inning home run gave us a lead against Houston in Game 4.

at ballparks over the years, but the last three games of this series were a tough act to equal, much less surpass. People in the stands were dancing and screaming and hugging each other, just as Lasorda was doing with his team in the clubhouse.

As tumultuous as this baseball season was, with the strike and two different halves, this sure was beginning to be a lot of fun. I even listened to the call-in shows on the radio while I drove home.

8

LEAGUE CHAMPIONSHIP SERIES

T he League Championship Series—also a best-of-five series— opened on October 13 with the Montreal Expos at Dodger Stadium and Ron Cey back in our lineup. The Penguin's broken flipper, protected now with only a plastic shield, had mended three weeks earlier than Dr. Frank Jobe's prognosis. Ron had convinced the Dodgers trainers and doctors that he was sufficiently healed and could play, but he was still going to be in some pain. He had been taking batting practice for a few days and appeared to be relatively pain free, but most of us knew that he wasn't. Even though he was still hurting and not at 100 percent, we were a better team with him.

Of course, we weren't the only ones riding a wave of momentum. In a season already deemed quirky because of the strike and the additional round of playoffs it spawned, the Expos did the unconventional: They fired manager Dick Williams with 26 games remaining in the season and replaced him with front-office executive Jim Fanning. Not only had Fanning not managed in 19 years, but the highest level he had reached as manager was Class-C. But the Expos were playing well under Fanning, having turned back the defending-champion Phillies in five games. The Expos were a talented team that featured Andre Dawson in the middle of the lineup, Gary Carter behind the plate, 12-game winner Steve Rogers anchoring their rotation, and a pesky, speedy leadoff hitter in Tim Raines, who proved to be the best rookie in the game that year not named Fernando Valenzuela.

I really thought that the Expos-Dodgers series was a more dramatic—and more difficult—series than what we endured in the World Series that year. I don't mean to discount the New York Yankees (okay, yes I do), but we were in for a real battle with the Expos.

"Yeah," agrees Steve Yeager, "We knew we had our hands full with the Expos, there's no doubt about that. … Montreal, with Steve Rogers on the mound, they were a threat. They were a good ball club, they had Andre Dawson and Gary Carter, and Tim Wallach was up there and Tim Raines was a rookie, so they had a good offensive club and defensive club. But I still say this: They talk about that home run that Kirk Gibson hit against the A's in the 1988 World Series, well that was dramatic. It was at Dodger Stadium and it won the game. But the home run Monday hit off Steve Rogers—that took us from one level to the next level. To me, it was the greatest moment in Dodger history."

More on that shortly, but first we have to get to Game 5.

GAME 1:
THE PENGUIN RETURNS

We went 5-2 against Montreal during the season, and it's probably safe to say we were a bit overconfident heading into the series—or at least suffering from some degree of letdown after the emotionally draining set with the Astros. But Cey's presence, as well as his bat, provided an immediate spark. He doubled in his first at-bat against Bill Gullickson, scoring Steve Garvey in the process, and scored later in the inning on Bill Russell's squeeze bunt, giving Burt Hooton a 2-0 lead after two innings.

Guerrero and Scioscia hit back-to-back homers off Expos ace reliever Jeff Reardon in the eighth inning, Steve Howe put out a fire in the ninth, and treated the home crowd of 51,000-plus to a 5-1 victory in the opener. Valenzuela was set to pitch Game 2 against Ray Burris, so the odds looked good for us to head to Montreal up by two games.

GAME 2:
RAY BURRIS?

That anticipated mismatch turned out the other way around, as the Expos got to Valenzuela early in the game, and Burris rolled for nine innings of shutout ball. The 3-0 loss tied the series as we headed to the frozen tundra of Quebec. We managed only five singles off Burris, while Fernando pitched what now would be considered a quality start, allowing three runs over six innings. But the Expos scored in the second inning on RBI hits from Warren Cromartie and Tim Raines and added another run in the sixth inning. Our best chance to pull off the come-from-behind victory occurred in the ninth inning when, with runners on first and second and one out, Pedro Guerrero lined into a game-ending double play.

The Expos probably took more out of this game than just a victory. It was the first time they had defeated us at Dodger Stadium in 11 tries. Dating back even further, we had taken 19 of the previous 20 played in Los Angeles. Would it give them a boost going back to their own ballpark? You better believe it would. They were going to be tough to beat at Stade Olympique.

NORTH OF THE BORDER

I remember on the way up to Montreal we kept hearing "The Happy Wanderer"—you know, "*val-deri, val-dera… .*" We read something in the paper along the lines of "those boys from Hollywood are not going to be able to take the cold weather." That was before the roof had been installed on Stade Olympique, or Olympic Stadium. The roof was still in storage over in France. And in our infinite wisdom, somebody brought up—and the rest of us dummies went along with—the idea to show the Expos how tough we were by leaving our jackets in the dugout when the teams were introduced on the field before the start of Game 3.

"That was my idea," says Lasorda. "One of the writers asked me if I was worried about playing in weather so cold that it might snow. I said, 'I'd be worried if it only snowed on our side of the field.' You look at that Montreal roster, all those guys came from Florida or California. What kind of advantage did they have? At least we had a Penguin on our team. So I told our guys, 'No jackets.' So Lopes says, 'But they're wearing jackets,' and I said, 'That's exactly the point. I want them to see that we're not going to let the weather beat us.' I think it made a big difference."

Maybe it did over the course of our games in Montreal, but as the 20-minute introduction ceremony dragged on, it didn't seem like such a brilliant move. We forgot how long we were going to be standing out there. They must have introduced everybody who ever attended a game in Montreal, and finally somebody said, "Whose idea was this? It was a bad one. Damn, it's cold out here!"

It wasn't freezing in Montreal, but as game time approached prior to Game 3 it was 46 degrees and falling—too cold to stand around with no jacket on. The Expos had Rogers on the mound, and all he'd done recently was outduel Steve Carlton twice in the Eastern Division playoff series. As a hitter, I didn't bother looking for a pitch above the belt buckle against Rogers. His sinker stayed down in the zone, and he tried to get ahead in the count early. Against lefties, he moved the ball

Not that he didn't enjoy it, but Tommy Lasorda often would argue with umpires just to take the heat off of his players. We were ready to argue with him after he sent us out on the field without our jackets in chilly weather for pregame introductions in Montreal.

in and out, and started quite a few breaking balls just off the plate outside, hoping the hitter would think it was outside and give up on it too early.

GAME 3:
MISTER ROGERS' NEIGHBORHOOD

Game 3 was more than just a matchup of exceptional Major League pitchers; it was a rematch of two guys—Steve Rogers and Jerry Reuss—who squared off against each other 15 years earlier in Missouri's high school state championship. Reuss got the best of Rogers as high schoolers, but Rogers beat us with ease on this chilly October day, 4-1. Our only run scored in the fourth inning after a pair of singles and a ground out plated Dusty Baker to give us a brief 1-0 lead. Jerry Reuss pitched his heart out for 5⅔ innings, but an Expos two-out rally in the sixth was capped by light-hitting Jerry White's decisive three-run homer.

In the ninth inning we got two runners on against Rogers for just the second time all game, but our threat was wiped out when Guerrero bounced into a double play with two on and no outs. Rogers held on by striking out Mike Scioscia to end the game, and the Expos were one win away from a trip to the World Series. By now, the Yankees had already swept the Oakland A's and were waiting to see who their next victim would be. Judging by the results of Game 3, it looked like they would prey on Montreal next.

A MAN, A TRENCHCOAT

You'd have to know Reuss to truly appreciate just how he reacted to this defeat. Following Game 3, the team went back to the hotel, and we were all upstairs in the bar looking playoff defeat in the face. Reuss excused himself and headed up a beautiful spiral staircase to the facilities. When he came back down, he had his trenchcoat on, but underneath, well, I'll let him explain it.

"You could see it in the eyes of everybody that there was way too much tension," recalls Reuss. "I even remember Reggie Smith saying, 'The hell with this, I'm going to New York anyway. Win or lose, I'm going to New York, and I'm going to enjoy myself.'

"After a few drinks, I had to make a deposit back into the Montreal system. And it was cold, and of course all of us dressed real well—coats and ties—and we had overcoats on because we had to wear them to and from the park and nobody had stopped by their rooms. Everyone just said, let's go on up and have a few and try to get this thing straightened out.

"It was a veteran ballclub, and guys would talk things out and veteran guys could take it. If somebody had something to say, you could say it, and nobody would take offense, because everybody had known each other a long enough time. There were no coaches, no managers, and no management in the bar—it was just players hashing it out, and the wives were there.

"So I went upstairs, and I don't know why I took my overcoat with me, but I did. And I was looking in the mirror and I thought, 'You know, this coat, it doesn't quite fit right. It's not quite long enough.' And, of course, being six foot five, I didn't buy it at the tall men's store. But I needed another opinion, and I figured, since these guys were being as honest as they possibly could be, then I figured somebody was going to give me another opinion when I went downstairs. So in order to accent the fact that I thought it was too small, I decided to take my trousers off and button up the overcoat and walk down this winding staircase in full view of everybody who was inside this fine establishment.

"… I've got to set the stage here: spotlights were on the stairs so you could see what you were doing, and I was thinking this is a perfect, Loretta Young-type moment. You remember Loretta Young, when she used to come down the staircase in this beautiful gown and make the announcement on what they were going to see on the show that night? I remember her from when I was a kid.

"Anyway, I figure I'm going to have that kind of moment. So I neatly folded my trousers, put them over my right arm and walked down the staircase with my sports coat and a tie and this overcoat and with my long socks and my pants carried over my arm. And I quietly walked over to my teammates and, straight-faced, looked at everybody and said, 'I think that this coat is too short. And since everybody's giving opinions around here, I thought I'd ask around the table whether you think this coat's too short or whether it's acceptable.' I can still hear the laughter. It just changed the whole tone of the room."

Yeager agrees.

"What Jerry did wasn't dirty or malicious or rotten or anything that would get us in trouble," recalls Yeager. "[He got the guys thinking], 'Let's go! Forget about this moping around here and feeling sorry for ourselves. We're better than this.' It was like a big kick in our rear end, so to speak."

We needed a little quirkiness to deal with stressful situations. But quirkiness alone wasn't going to dig us out of our second hole of the playoffs. Garvey used to say that you needed three basic attributes to win a World Series: experience, pride, and enough ego to believe you can do anything. Dusty, for one, had a little of that needed ego.

"I remember showing up for Game 4," remembers Baker, "and we had to wear a suit on travel days. And so the team said, 'After the game, if we lose, we're going back home.' So I didn't come to the park in a suit. I told my wife I wasn't going home. I was going to the World Series no matter what. They said, 'Where's your suit?' And I said, 'Oh, no. We're coming back tomorrow. We're going to win.'"

After Reuss's comedic exploit the previous night, we snapped out of our pity party and headed back to Olympic Stadium for Game 4 with an even more determined attitude. But questions still lingered, very quietly in the backs of our minds, or at least in mine. I wondered whether this would be it for the '81 Dodgers, and if so, who would be back next year? I sent these distractions to my "mental trashcan." We all have that receptacle. Whenever you have an odd thought, you immediately banish it to the "trashcan."

One of the greatest gifts most good athletes have, besides God-given ability, is the uncanny knack to block out thoughts that don't have a darn thing to do with hitting, fielding, throwing, or winning. An athlete's ability to focus is amazing.

GAME 4: COMEBACK II

We would need to do a lot of things exceptionally well if we were going to return for a Game 5. And we did. Hooton took the ball for us on three days' rest with temperatures in the forties against Bill Gullickson. You couldn't tell by the final score, 7-1, but this game was a nail-biting pitchers duel. A Larry Parrish error led to Baker's RBI double in the third inning, which plated a single run. A Cey error opened the door for the Expos to tie it with an unearned run on Cromartie's fourth-inning single.

The game remained knotted at 1-1 as the starters dueled into the eighth. In the Dodgers half of the eighth, Baker singled with one out, and Garvey followed with a home run off Gullickson to put us up 3-1. The Expos tried to mount a comeback in their half of the eighth, putting a pair on with one out. But Lasorda relieved Hooton with Bob Welch, who squashed the Expos' threat.

We blew the game open in the ninth inning on a two-run single by Baker with the bases loaded and RBI hits from Cey and Smith. Steve Howe slammed the door shut, tying the series again with an all-or-nothing Game 5 set for the next day.

This team continued to amaze me with its ability to rise to the occasion time after time. We were either a very tough group in our mental makeup, or we were just too stubborn to accept that we were up against tough odds.

The question after Game 4 was whether Reuss should perform an encore on the spiral staircase in the hotel bar. We decided Jerry could have the night off, and we would all get a lot of rest instead. The next day, my first thoughts were this: we lost to the Yankees in '77, we lost to the Yankees in '78, and by God, somebody's going to face them. It had better be us. It was a sleepless night, as I pondered writing a new chapter in the Yankees-Dodgers rivalry book.

SNOWED OUT

The weather that greeted us that Sunday morning was miserable. It was raining with some snowflakes mixed in. Fernando was sitting in the Dodger dugout for a few minutes collecting his thoughts and watching the precipitation fall, all the while seeming to enjoy watching his breath in the bitterly cold air. I asked him if he had ever seen snow before and he told me in Spanish, "*Si, en las montanas,*" or "Yes, in the mountains." Heck, all season long he'd handled everything like a seasoned veteran, why not the rain and snow, too! In light of everything else we had seen him do, he could probably ski around the bases if he had to!

The game was delayed. One hour, two hours, three hours. Finally, at 7:30 p.m., three and a half hours past the scheduled starting time and more than six hours after fans had entered the stadium, the fifth and deciding game of the series was postponed. The game to decide the National League Champions would be played the following day at 1:30 p.m. The winner would go to New York to play the Yankees in the World Series with Game 1 scheduled for Tuesday night.

I wondered where that "mental trashcan" was right then.

GAME 5:
EVERY KID'S DREAM

I had a good feeling as soon as I saw the crowd at Olympic Stadium for the rescheduled game—because there really wasn't one. Only 36,491 people showed up for the Monday game, so the cavernous stadium was far from full. With 20,000 fewer people in attendance than for either of the previous two games, I had to wonder whether baseball was that important to the people of Montreal. I don't mean to sound harsh, but a trip to the World Series was on the line. It gave our team a bit of a mental boost, as if some of the hostility of the home crowd had been sucked out of the stadium.

The only time I ever lost sight of the flight of a home-run ball was the biggest home run I ever hit. I never saw this one off Steve Rogers until Andre Dawson stopped running in right-center field and the ball landed in the stands.

Reuss agrees: "It was in the daytime and the sun was shining, so there was a little bit of warmth. …It was just a different feel, and it was unlike the first couple of days. I could sense that the momentum had shifted."

I remember thinking in the clubhouse before the game that we had nothing to lose in one sense, and everything to lose in another. Our season was possibly just 27 outs away from ending if we didn't find a way to pull off a victory. Game 5 was a rematch of Game 2, the 20-year-old Valenzuela versus Burris. We hoped the outcome wouldn't be the same.

Raines opened the first inning for the Expos with a double, and scored on a double-play ball to give Montreal the early lead. But Valenzuela kept the Expos in check for the next three innings until he could do some damage himself—with a bat. With Guerrero on first and me on third and one out in the fifth, Fernando grounded out to drive me in and tie the game.

That's how the score remained into the ninth inning—still tied at one—when Fanning felt Burris had tired and switched to his ace, Rogers, who got two quick outs. I stepped to the plate with Guerrero on deck. Rogers kept pitching me away, away, and he fell behind in the count, 3-1, forcing him to give me a pitch that I could handle. He had to want that pitch more outside, but it got a lot of the plate and I crushed it to the right-center gap. Dawson chased after it, but I knew he wasn't going to catch it. As the ball cleared the fence, I had just passed first base and was heading to second. I threw my left arm into the air and continued my jog around the bases, jumping a little when I got to home plate. My teammates beat the heck out of me, which I thought was a little premature, because the Expos had the heart of their order due up in the bottom of the ninth.

Freddy returned to the mound and made quick work of Rodney Scott and Dawson. Then he issued his second and third walks of the game to Gary Carter—who was lifted for a pinch-runner—and Larry Parrish. Lasorda was faced with a tough call with Jerry White, who had homered in Game 3, stepping to the plate: stick with the rookie

Bob Welch, who got the save in relief of Fernando Valenzuela during Game 5 of the League Championship Series, celebrates with Steve Garvey after the game's final out.

phenom or go to the bullpen for Bobby Welch. A lot of people might not remember, but Tommy actually took Freddy out of the game, and the move paid off. Welch got a ground ball out of White. Lopes fielded the ball, tossed to Garvey, and we were going to New York for the third time in five years!

I'd be lying if I said that I didn't then—or don't now—get immense satisfaction knowing that I played a role in helping us win that game and get to the World Series. But let's not forget the guy on the mound was the same guy who nobody really knew on Opening Day, the guy who rewrote the record books as a rookie and was still there on the mound, pitching into the ninth inning in the game to decide whether we'd reach the World Series. A tip of the cap is due to Fernando.

"I think that Fernando held his composure as well as anybody for a young kid," says Yeager. "I mean, he held his composure like a veteran holds it, if not better. Of course, Tommy made the change to go to Welchy, but Fernando learned to play the game with a bunch of older, veteran players in Mexico and situations like that that came up didn't bother him like it would bother some young kids today, or even some veterans.

"… But Fernando just went out and did what he had to do. And I think that his attitude was that 'I know I can get you out, and I have a defense behind me, and all you have to do is hit the ball at one of them and I'll get you out.' His composure was outstanding."

Our composure took a back seat to the celebration on the field and in the clubhouse. The Happy Wanderers were headed to the World Series for a rematch with those *damn* Yankees.

Val-deri, val-dera … that.

9

WORLD SERIES

S teve Yeager and I had been through a lot together, including losing two World Series to the Yankees prior to 1981. I remember during one of those losing years, there were around 150 uniformed New York City police officers surrounding our team bus as we prepared to depart from Yankee Stadium. And yet the Yankees fans were allowed to come right up to the bus and rock it back and forth. The cops did nothing. We were in hostile territory. And that was just the way it was when you played the Yankees in the World Series. You were never going to get the benefit of the doubt. You were going to have to earn it, and then some.

Possibly, Steve and I had "earning it" on our minds as we headed out to dinner together after clinching the NL pennant against Montreal. Upon being seated at the restaurant, he proposed a toast that I will never forget: "Roomie," he said to me, "here's to a home run in the World Series." And I replied: "Before this is all over, you are going to be the toast of the town."

Turns out, we did a good job of telling the future that night. Upon completion of the World Series, Yeager was named one of three MVPs in the World Series, in part because of not one, but *two* home runs he hit against New York.

But before we celebrate the ending, let's build up to the climactic finish.

WELCOME TO THE BIG APPLE

Upon our arrival in New York City for Game 1 of the World Series, the *Today Show* requested Tommy Lasorda and me to join Bryant Gumble on the air to talk about the World Series that would start that night at Yankee Stadium. The limo arrived at our hotel very early to take us over to the studio. We waited for a while in the "green room" before finally joining Bryant on the set to do a live segment. The conversation started with a discussion of the playoff series we had just captured against the Expos and, in particular, about the home run I had hit in the ninth inning of Game 5 to clinch the series.

Tommy was at his best, boiling over with enthusiasm and preaching like a reverend in church about his team overcoming tremendous odds to finally reach the "Fall Classic." Tommy and I had known Gumble since his days as a sportscaster in Los Angeles, and Bryant used that association to perfection. He had Tommy ranting and raving about the Dodgers having another opportunity to face the Yankees. Hell, Tommy was even making a strong case for New Yorkers to root for the Dodgers!

Eventually, Bryant pointed to the monitor and said he would like my opinion on some of the Yankees we would face in the World Series. The first Yankee to appear on the screen was third baseman Graig Nettles, who almost single-handedly ruined our chances to score runs with his spectacular defense in our previous meetings. "He can't possibly play any better," I answered. "We just need to hit the ball to somebody different than him." The next face to appear was no surprise either: Reggie Jackson. "This is the year we have to stop him," I said.

This continued for a couple more minutes; a different Yankee player would pop up on the monitor to elicit a response, and I would provide a few words about each. Until the last face was put up on the screen: George Steinbrenner's mug! I looked at the picture, looked at Bryant and Tommy, and then bit my tongue and simply answered: "He will not get one hit for the Yankees and will not be a factor."

Man, the things I wanted to say, but I'm glad I just left it at that. The limo ride delivered us back to the hotel and it was time for me to get a nap. Tommy, on the other hand, hit the ground running and disappeared. I would see him later at Yankee Stadium.

The New York newspapers wrote their preview stories for this World Series as if they expected a replay of the 1977 and 1978 World Series. According to them, we didn't match up favorably with the Yankees at even one position. In this town, we were perceived as just another team being brought in to feed the appetite of the Yankee Dynasty. Gee, and all this time I thought we had a pretty good team. I'm glad the "experts" set me straight before the World Series started so I wouldn't get my hopes too high!

BAD BREAK FOR BAKE

We did catch one break when Reggie Jackson, Mr. October, wasn't in the starting lineup for Game 1 because of a pulled calf muscle. But we weren't exactly at full strength, either.

"I sure wasn't," recalls Dusty Baker. "I didn't contribute in that World Series, although not too many people ever knew why. I got in a fight after the last game in Montreal with some Canadian dudes in the parking lot. So I got on the plane and my hand was throbbing, and I told Tommy, 'I think I broke my hand.' And he said, 'What?' And I called my dad and he told me, 'I told you about fighting.' So I went to a doctor the morning of Game 1 and the doctor told me, 'Yeah, well, you need about six weeks for your hand to heal.' Six weeks?

"So I went to [coach] Manny Mota, and Manny let me use one of those bowling sleeves that he used to use (to stabilize the wrist). And people were asking me, 'Are you choking, or what's going on?' My friends were calling me [after seeing me in Game 1], saying, 'You're missing pitches.' I told them, 'Man, I've got a bad hand, but I can't tell nobody.'

"But Tommy said, 'No, you've got to play, Dusty, you've got to be on the field as a threat. But you can't tell nobody, because then they're going to pitch around somebody else to get to you.'

"I'm glad we won more than anything, because had we lost, then I would've felt directly responsible for not being able to play to my ability."

A MATCHUP OR MISMATCH?

The Yankees were solid favorites in Las Vegas. Like us, they led their division at the time of the strike. They beat the Milwaukee Brewers in the first round of the playoffs and then swept the Oakland Athletics in the second round, so they were well rested compared to us. This would be the 11th World Series meeting between the Dodgers and Yankees—no other two teams have met so frequently— and the Yankees held an 8-2 edge in the competition.

Without the benefit of a workout day for preparation, we had a brief pregame meeting to go over our scouting reports on the Yankees. We addressed their hitters and pitchers, their tendencies, who was hot and who was not—all the normal stuff compiled by the Dodgers' outstanding advance scouts. The Yankees, as we learned, had held meetings while waiting for the outcome of our series with the Expos. They were forced to review both the Expos and Dodgers, not knowing until the previous night which team they would face.

Dave Winfield was quoted as saying the only difference in playing against the Expos or Dodgers would be "what coat we're taking out of the cleaners—are we taking fur or cotton/polyester?" Dave evidently led a different type of lifestyle than the rest of us. I was worrying about

Reggie Jackson (left) was already a feared hitter, and Pedro Guerrero was in the process of becoming one, when the two met during the 1981 World Series.

the pitchers we'd be facing in the upcoming games, and he was worrying about the weather of the host city and how that might affect his wardrobe.

Our real strength in 1981 was pitching, but the Yankees had a good staff to match ours. Veteran lefthander Ron Guidry was eligible to be a free agent and had pitched well in his "walk year," posting an 11-5 record with a 2.76 ERA. He was possibly making his last start or two in pinstripes. After a so-so first half, he had rebounded after the strike with a 6-2 record and had a miniscule 1.74 ERA. The only recent blemish for Guidry was that he was roughed up a little bit in his two starts against Milwaukee in the first round of the playoffs.

Lefthander Tommy John, another veteran at age 38, pitched for the Dodgers prior to signing with the Yankees as a free agent, so we knew about his "sinker" and curveball. What we didn't know was if he still used the same brand of sandpaper. Tommy had posted a 2.63 ERA that year for the Yankees, and picked up a big victory in the opening game of the league playoffs against the A's after failing to win a game over his final four regular-season starts. When he pitched, he kept his team in the game with a chance to win, as evidenced by the fact that he pitched seven of the Yankees' 16 complete games in 1981.

Yet another lefthander, Dave Righetti, had been the team's most consistent pitcher since his call-up from the Minor Leagues in May. The 22-year-old rookie, who went 8-4 with a 2.05 ERA during the regular season, earned three of the Yankees' six postseason wins over the first two rounds, allowing just one run in 15 innings. He was on the "hot" list.

The Yankees bullpen was equally potent, especially with hard-throwing Goose Gossage waiting for a chance to close out a game. During the 1981 season Gossage posted a ridiculous 0.77 ERA in 32 appearances. The rest of the New York pen was almost as stingy.

The Yankees lineup was potent, as usual. They balanced home run hitters like Winfield, Jackson, Nettles, and Oscar Gamble with contact hitters like Lou Piniella, Jerry Mumphrey, and Willie Randolph. It was Jerry Reuss's job to try to stifle them in Game 1.

"It was my first trip to Yankee Stadium," recalls Reuss. "And what people say is true: that first trip to Yankee Stadium is a little breathtaking, because you are walking into history. You can sense it, you can smell it, you can feel it. You add all of that to the fact that it's your first trip to the World Series, which affects veterans and rookies alike. Then add to that that it's a Dodgers-Yankees World Series. It had a whole different perspective from anything that I had experienced in my previous 11 years in the big leagues."

That's an understatement. For the visiting team, playing at Yankee Stadium feels like the gladiators of old Roman times—in this case the visiting team—are facing off against the lions—the Yankees. We sure felt like we had been fed to the lions there on a couple of occasions. That said, at least we were more confident about our chances this time than when we came into Yankee Stadium in 1977 and 1978.

It had been three years since most of us had played in a World Series game at Yankee Stadium, but it didn't take long for us to rediscover the seemingly always-present New York City hospitality in Game 1 of the series.

GAME 1: THEY STILL LOOK LIKE THE YANKEES

Graig Nettles was up to his old tricks at third base, sucking up base hits and turning them into outs. He made two defensive plays that looked like carbon copies of three stops he had made to help turn the 1978 World Series in the Yankees' favor. We didn't agree with at least one call from the umpires. And Dusty Baker had a Coke bottle thrown at him by a fan in left field. It just whizzed past his shoulder during the game. Lasorda threatened to pull the whole team off the field in protest, but that wouldn't have changed the score. We were in for yet another warm reception in Yankee Stadium.

Reuss was a money pitcher if you ask me, but he had already pitched three times in 10 days, and the Yankees hit him early and often. Jerry, it turned out, was indeed a little bit overwhelmed by the moment. The Yankees had succeeded in knocking him out of the game in a hurry.

First baseman Bob Watson let Reuss know what facing the Yankees in the World Series was all about. After a first-inning single by Mumphrey and a double by Piniella, Watson hit a three-run homer to put the Yankees on the board in a big way. After our 5-3 loss, Watson said he had always wanted to be a Dodger, having grown up in Los Angeles. But that was when Lasorda was a scout, and he didn't sign Watson out of Fremont High School. Watson said he never forgot it and hoped that one day he could punish Tommy for that. Nice going, 'Sorda. Watson said he was thrilled when Reuss pitched to him in that situation with first base open.

Piniella knocked Reuss out of the game with an RBI single in the third inning. The line for Reuss was not pretty: four runs and five hits allowed, including the homer to Watson, in two-plus innings of work. Reliever Bobby Castillo didn't fare much better. In one inning of work, he walked five batters, including three straight to allow the Yankees another run in the fourth inning.

Obviously, we were hoping for better results against the Yankees this time around, but if it were not for the calendar indicating this was indeed 1981, we would have been hard-pressed not to believe we had just gone through some type of a time warp back to 1977 or '78.

Offensively, we couldn't get to Guidry but once in seven innings, when Yeager made good on his fortune-telling by hitting a towering solo homer in the fifth inning. We made a sincere effort to take the game back from the Yankees bullpen in the eighth inning. After a pair of walks, Gossage was called upon to face pinch-hitter Jay Johnstone, who responded with an RBI single. Baker followed with a sacrifice fly to score a second run. With Johnstone in scoring position, Garvey's line-drive bid for extra bases was intercepted by a diving Graig Nettles and his Gold Glove, halting our comeback in its tracks. Gossage took care of business in the ninth, and the Yankees held on to win 5-3.

"Guidry, of course, was used to the pressure because he'd been through the Series against the Dodgers in those two years, '77 and '78, and it was his home turf," recalls Reuss. "He outpitched me. I got a couple pitches up in the first inning and they just got whacked. And we had to play catch-up after that. I sat there after the ball game and went over the pitches, pretty much pitch by pitch, and I said, 'I've got to change some things, make some adjustments, and if I get another chance in this series, I'm going to do just that.'"

GAME 2:
TOMMY JOHN OPERATES

We sent Burt Hooton to the mound in Game 2 of the best-of-seven series, and New York countered with Tommy John, the man with the bionic arm. Both starters threw zeroes up on the board until the Yankees scored a single, unearned run in the fifth inning. Randolph led off the inning by reaching on a Davey Lopes error, one of six errors the Dodger second baseman committed in the series. Randolph was knocked in by a double off the bat of shortstop Larry Milbourne.

Meanwhile, we couldn't do much with T.J.'s sinkerball, and his infield gobbled up our grounders. We managed just four singles in the game. The Yankees tacked on two more runs in the eighth against Steve Howe and Dave Stewart, and Gossage picked up the save for the home team.

With the 3-0 loss, we were right back in a familiar place: facing long odds in a short series. I like to think that by needing to mount a comeback for the third consecutive series, we had the Yankees right where we wanted them. But the rest of the baseball world didn't see it that way.

"A sportswriter came up to me and said, 'Reggie Jackson was just saying that you're going to have to win four in a row to beat them,'" remembers Baker. "And I said, 'That's all we need, a math major.'"

In reality, we had to win four of the next five games or we'd wind up with the same results as in 1977 and 1978, watching the Yankees celebrate winning the world championship. In the 78-year history of the Series, 34 teams had been in this position—down two games to none—and only seven came back to win it all. Ironically, the last team to do so was the Yankees, in 1978 against us!

To make matters worse, we were reminded that dating back to the 1978 World Series, the Yankees had beaten us in six consecutive games. I was in need of my "mental trashcan" in a big way. But that year, the Dodgers became accustomed to living the underdog life. The truth is, having already come back from the brink of elimination twice, we were feeling pretty comfortable in the role.

"The Yankees were in the driver's seat and everybody was writing us off before the series even started," recalls Garvey. "But even though we lost the first two games, when we went home we had a lot of confidence, it really was like we had them where we wanted them."

Bill Russell agrees: "Even though we were down the first two games, I just felt that the confidence was still there. We felt that, what we'd gone through, it was just a feeling that we're going to prevail here—things are going to turn our way here for a change."

GAME 3:
PENGUIN SAVES FERNANDO

I think most people involved with baseball hope for games that are not decided by an error, a controversial call, or an injury. Most want a game that is clean of any debate or controversy, decided on the field by the expected participants. Unfortunately for the Yankees, as the series progressed, injuries became a factor with some of their key players. Nettles seriously jammed his thumb diving for a Bill Russell grounder in Game 2. Reggie Jackson did some light running in the outfield at Dodger Stadium on the travel day between Games 2 and 3 to test his strained left calf. Neither player would appear in Game 3, which pitted two rookie pitchers—our Valenzuela and their Dave Righetti.

The fact that we were sending a 20-year-old to the mound, and the Yankees were sending a 22-year-old, was a tribute to each team's scouting departments. It was the scouts who discovered them and recognized their potential as Major League pitchers. General managers make the trades and tweak the rosters, field managers develop the players and strategize how to win games, but it's the scouts who discover or ignore the talent.

The Valenzuela-Righetti matchup marked only the fourth time in 78 years that rookie pitchers had opposed each other as starters in a World Series game. Ironically, each could have been wearing the other team's uniform had front-office decisions gone differently. Fernando, still a teenager pitching in Mexico, had been pursued by a Yankee scout, and Righetti was close to being dealt to the Dodgers in 1980, but the Yankees turned down a deal for the Dodgers' Don Sutton. Fernando had been prominent on the Dodgers' radar since he was 17, when scout Corito Verona first submitted a report on him. Soon after, Dodger scout Mike Brito wrote that Fernando had "a chance" to make it to the big leagues. But in the 1981 World Series, he had his work cut out for him.

We got Freddy three quick runs in the first inning, as Penguin slugged a three-run homer off a low fastball from Righetti, who had allowed only one home run all regular season in 105 innings pitched. Three runs with Valenzuela on the mound seemed like money in the bank, but these were the Yankees, and this was the World Series. Nothing would come easily.

Valenzuela wasn't sharp. He gave up homers to Watson in the second inning and Rick Cerone in the third inning, and just that fast we were trailing, 4-3. George Frazier took over for Righetti in the third after the struggling starter allowed the first two batters to reach base.

Garvey singled to start the fifth, and Cey followed with a walk. Guerrero followed by chopping a double over the third baseman's head, scoring Garvey on the play. I was walked intentionally to load the bases, and that was all she wrote for Frazier. Rudy May came into the game and coerced Scioscia into hitting a bouncing double-play ball that scored Cey and moved Guerrero to third. Lasorda now had a decision to make. We had regained the lead, 4-3, but Fernando was at the plate with two outs and a runner on third. Tommy decided to allow him to hit, and Valenzuela grounded out to the shortstop to end the inning. It seemed like a gutsy move at the time, but it proved to be the right call in the end.

"It wasn't really a pretty game for Fernando," recalls Cey. "But as he certainly did throughout his career for us and the Dodgers, when he was scheduled to pitch, he pitched—and no one else was going to get the ball. He battled and finished up strong."

Fernando faced the minimum over the next two innings, and we took our one-run lead into the eighth inning, which led to the single-most important play of the entire series. Third baseman Aurelio Rodriguez, playing for the injured Nettles, singled to start the inning. Milbourne followed with a single, which brought veteran Bobby Murcer to the plate to hit for the pitcher.

With two on, nobody out, and Valenzuela having already walked seven, Murcer was asked to bunt, but he flubbed it and hit a soft pop-up down the third-base line. Cey, only weeks removed from suffering a broken arm, charged down the line and made a diving catch in foul territory right before the ball hit the ground. He scrambled to his feet and threw over a ducking Valenzuela to Lopes, who was covering first, to double up Milbourne. With a new life, Fernando got Randolph to ground out on a fielder's choice to end the inning.

In the ninth, Valenzuela, who logged 145 pitches in the game, held on for a 5-4 complete-game win by striking out Piniella on a screwball to end the game. The tension must have been building, because our rookie reliever, Alejandro Peña, had to be hospitalized with a bleeding ulcer.

GAME 4:
REGGIE FIT, WE'RE TIED

Reggie Jackson returned for Game 4, which turned into a slugfest. Lasorda started Bobby Welch, deciding to save Reuss, Hooton, and Valenzuela for the final three games if the series went seven. But Welch's workday was a short one, 16 pitches and no outs to be exact. With the bases loaded and one run in, Lasorda brought in Dave Goltz, who put that inning down after allowing another run to score on a sacrifice fly. Goltz allowed single runs in each of the next two innings to give the Yankees a 4-0 lead heading into the bottom of the third inning.

We cut the deficit in half in the third, as pinch-hitter Ken Landreaux doubled to lead off the inning and was singled in by Lopes. After a Garvey single, Cey's groundout scored Lopes. We further trimmed the lead to 4-3 in the fifth when Garvey doubled and was singled home by Cey.

The Yankees came roaring back in the sixth to score a pair of unearned runs off Tom Niedenfuer in the sixth after Russell's error allowed Randolph to reach base safely to start the inning. New York's lead was extended to 6-3, but in case people weren't paying attention, we weren't going away quietly. In the bottom of the sixth we responded in a big way. Johnstone's two-run pinch-hit homer off Ron Davis may have been the biggest hit of the series as it energized our team and rattled—at least temporarily—the Yankees.

Reggie Jackson reached base all five times he stepped to the plate in Game 4, but with no designated hitter in the National League ballpark, the Yankees couldn't hide his glove. Lopes followed Johnstone's home run with a routine fly ball toward Jackson in right field, but Reggie lost it in the L.A. haze and the ball clanked off his glove as Lopes reached second. Russell singled home Lopes on an 0-2 pitch, and the game was tied.

In the seventh inning against new Yankee reliever Frazier, I hit a ball to right-center that Mumphrey couldn't quite get to. That advanced Baker, who had singled in front of me, to third while I ended up with a double. The Yankees intentionally walked Guerrero to load the bases with no one out, and Bob Lemon, looking for a ground-ball double play, brought in Tommy John. Yeager, pinch-hitting for Scioscia, had other ideas, and hit a sacrifice fly to right field to give us the lead. After a Steve Howe sacrifice bunt moved the runners to second and third with two outs, Lopes hit a chopper toward third that eluded the infielders and gave us a precious insurance run and an 8-6 lead.

"Mr. October," Reggie Jackson, homered off Steve Howe in the eighth inning to make it a one-run game. Then with two on and two out in the ninth, Howe slammed the door on the Yankees by getting Randolph to fly out to Derrel Thomas to end the game. Howe pitched three innings of relief to pick up the win.

The series was tied at two games each. After 15 runs, 27 hits, and 22 stranded runners, we had come off the mat again to even the series. We truly believed we were on our way to another remarkable comeback, and that notion was supported by an uncharacteristic doom-and-gloom comment from Gossage to reporters in the Yankees clubhouse after the game.

"We stunk," he said. "I was warming up in the ninth inning, and I threw one clear over the (bullpen) fence. Not just barely over the fence, but about five feet over. I said, 'Geez, don't put me in there.' That stuff rubs off."

GAME 5:
WE TAKE THE LEAD AND
HOLD OUR BREATH

Momentum was ours as the series headed into Game 5, the final game we would play at home. Reuss and Guidry hooked up in a better-pitched rematch of Game 1. In retrospect, I just knew something big might happen with Jerry on the mound on that day. Something about the way he was going about his business prior to the game made me think we were in for a treat. Baseball players are, for the most part at least, creatures of habit, and being around one another for as many months of the year as we are, you can usually spot something in the mannerisms of your teammates that aren't quite the same as you normally see.

Jerry was normally very intense on the days he pitched, but on this day the intensity level was just about to leap totally off the Richter scale. He seemed to be in a different world than the rest of us. As I said earlier, we all knew how good Jerry was when he pitched against us, we just didn't know if he was aware of his own talent. Prior to Game 5, he looked like he certainly had a clue.

The Yankees struck first, turning Jackson's second-inning double and a Lopes error into a run, and Guidry made it stand up through six innings. Guidry was cruising along, and so Lemon stuck with him at a time when he usually would have gone to the bullpen. The bottom of the seventh might have been the half-inning that swung the Series.

Per Lasorda's request, Baker was succeeding in playing through his injury without tipping off the Yankees. It was a struggle for him every game, and he was missing pitches that he would normally hit hard enough to live up to his nickname, "Dr. Scald." But he never let his injury detract from his intensity level. Dusty didn't know it at the time, but when he struck out against Guidry to start the seventh inning, he might have actually helped us win the game.

Dusty struck out while over-swinging at a Guidry pitch. Lasorda recognized the aggressive approach at the plate, and gave some advice to Guerrero and Yeager, the two hitters who were scheduled up next. Lasorda knew that with Goose Gossage warming in the bullpen, now was our best chance to get another run on the board. Guerrero had struck out his last time up, missing the pitch badly. Tommy called both Guerrero and Yeager over to his seat in the dugout, and instructed them to "take a nice and easy swing." After missing one fastball, Guerrero paid attention to his manager's advice, and smoked a slider into the leftfield pavilion for a game-tying home run.

Guerrero said afterward: "I'd been swinging hard—too hard. [Tommy] just told me to try and make contact and go with the pitch, and that's what I did. [Guidry] was throwing the slider in the dirt all day and we were swinging at it. I just waited for a good pitch."

Yeager was on deck and didn't even see Guerrero's home run because he had bent over to retrieve the weighted donut in the on-deck circle. He did remember that he'd taken Guidry deep in the first game on a 1-2 fastball, and when this at-bat reached the same count,

Here's my roomie, Steve Yeager, taking a curtain call after his Game 5 World Series home run.

Yeager was ready for the same pitch. Sure enough, the waist-high fastball came down the pipe, and Yeager deposited it in the stands.

The 2-1 score would hold until Reuss was able to finish off the Yankees in the ninth, allowing just five hits on the night. But the game's conclusion was not without its unforgettable moments.

A SICKENING SOUND

Afternoon games at most stadiums are extremely pleasant to play and watch, until the late afternoon sun begins to set and casts dark shadows onto the field. Then it becomes an adventure to follow the flight of the baseball, especially if it's traveling over 90 miles per hour at your head.

In the bottom of the eighth inning, with the shadows having already swallowed up the Dodger Stadium infield, Goose Gossage relieved Guidry. Facing Cey with a runner on second and two outs, Gossage let a 94-mile-per-hour fastball get away. Penguin froze at the plate, and the ball made contact with his helmet near his left temple, where his helmet—which did not have an ear flap—rested above his ear. The ball striking Cey's helmet made the most sickening sound I've ever heard. Ron just crumpled at home plate as his helmet flew in one direction and the ball in another. You could hear the entire stadium gasp in horror. We just hoped Ron wasn't dead.

"When you hear the whack and you see him kicking his feet on the ground, you think, 'Gosh, this guy's going through convulsions out there,'" recalls Russell. "It was a scary thing to see a guy get hit like that. I remember in the Minor Leagues I got hit like that once and I was done for a week. It just brought back memories."

The Dodger Stadium crowd went silent. Teammates were horrified. Cey never seemed to lose consciousness, though, and while lying in the dirt, he grabbed his head.

"It was a blur," Cey recalls. "All I did was kind of tilt my head downward at the last minute, because I was really trying to stay on this pitch as long I could. The ball just disappeared at some point. So I just

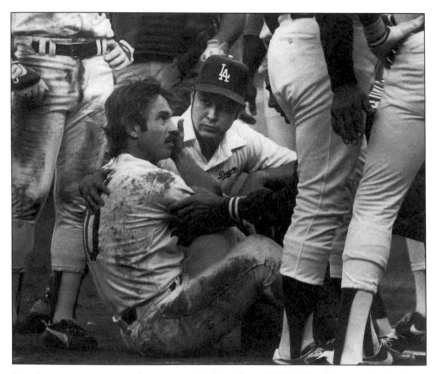

Ron Cey receives attention from trainers Paul Padilla and Bill Buhler (obscured) after being beaned in the helmet by a Goose Gossage fastball in Game 5 of the World Series.

decided to duck down a little bit and that's really what saved me. If I had gone the other way—if I had moved probably a quarter of an inch—instead of the ball striking the helmet it hits the side of my temple. Who knows what happens then? But the helmet saved me.

"I remember falling in slow motion. I remember (trainer) Bill Buhler coming out to home plate and I had my hands wrapped around my head. Basically I can't see anything. And Bill's taking a look, and I said, 'Bill, is anything sticking out of my head? Does it look okay?' And I got up towards the end and they walked me in and waited until after the game to have a CAT scan and all of that. Everything came out okay, but it was a scary moment. And I was fortunate that I didn't get a more severe injury like Tony Conigliaro, because then you're talking about [the ending of] a career, instead of missing a couple days."

Tests at a local hospital turned up only a concussion. We were excited to regain the lead in the series, but the frightening sight of Cey going down put a damper on our postgame celebration. George Steinbrenner wasn't too happy after the game, either. "The Boss" allegedly had a rumble in an elevator at the club hotel, claiming he was defending his team and its city. Instead of going back to New York with a World Series trophy, all he had was a sore hand and a swollen lip. We were only one win away from holding that trophy, but we would have to win it in Yankee Stadium.

"After we won the first two games in L.A., we started thinking that maybe it was our turn," says Garvey. "And when Reuss pitched that third game in L.A. and we won it for a sweep at home, the Yankees were back on their heels and we had the momentum. I can't remember a group that had as much confidence as we did, heading back to New York."

PRAYING FOR RON AND RAIN

We flew to New York on the Monday off day and woke up Tuesday for Game 6 with the realization that this could be a historic day for the Dodgers organization—*if* we played our best game of the year. But somebody forgot to tell the weatherman. New York was cold and rainy, and it didn't look like a game of baseball was in the plans.

One player in particular was hoping the game would be cancelled. Cey, still woozy from the Gossage fastball that scrambled his brain, knew there was no way he would be able to play if the game was held. It was some time during the early afternoon hours that the players' hotel room phones began to ring. The message was from the Dodgers' traveling secretary, Billy DeLury (the best in baseball, I might add) informing us that the game had been postponed a day.

The down time for me was spent reading *New York Times* baseball writer Murray Chass's story about George's meeting with his team the day before in Los Angeles:

> *George Steinbrenner, the Yankees principal owner and principal igniter of the Yankee winning streaks, says he has addressed his team for the last time this year.*
>
> *"I'm through," said Steinbrenner, who spoke to his players before today's fifth game of the World Series. "I've said all I'm going to say. They understand what they have to do. I don't think they want to be an embarrassment to New York. That's why I'm so cocky and sure we're going to win. But some guys are going to have to start doing it instead of talking about it."*

An "embarrassment to New York?" Thank *God* for Peter O'Malley! Meanwhile, Cey was thanking divine intervention for an extra day of recuperation.

"When I heard the game was canceled, I just said, 'Thank God,' because there's absolutely no way I could've played that day," Cey remembers. "The next day I went out early to Central Park just to get my mind straight. And I got to the ballpark around 1:30 in the afternoon, and it was cold. I went out, did a workout, ran and threw, and when the team got to Yankee Stadium, Tommy made out the lineup. He left the fourth spot open and said to me, 'Let me know.' I said, 'Well, everything's fine right now, but I've got to hit and take ground balls and I'll let you know as soon as I can.'

"Tommy was watching me and hounding me, 'How're you feeling now?' 'I'm doing fine, just leave me alone. Get out of here!' And then he came up to the batting cage and said, 'How's it going? How do you feel? What do you think?' And I said, 'I'm not done with batting practice yet. When we're done, I'll come and see you.'

"I was feeling pretty good, but I just wanted to make sure that when I got back into the clubhouse I was 100 percent sure that I could go. So I walked in and gave him the high-five, and he plugged my name in the lineup."

We all knew that Cey was playing on guts, something he had already proven he had plenty of. He eventually took himself out of the game because of dizziness, but he gave us all a huge lift just by getting his name on the lineup card. Forty-eight hours before we thought he might be dead.

Russell, who worked alongside Cey for nearly a decade, wasn't quite sure Cey was as close to 100 percent as he claimed.

"I kept looking at him and talking to him over there and his eyes were a little glassy, but I didn't know if it was the cold weather or from getting hit," says Russell. "I gave him the benefit of the doubt. I knew that all the years we'd played together, we had played hurt. I knew that nothing was going to keep him out of this game and this series."

Before Game 6 started, we had to put the memories of 1977 and 1978 out of our minds, a tough task with 50,000 Yankees fans reminding you every minute of the way. As we were introduced on the foul lines prior to the game, though, the stadium was rather quiet— no thunderous crowd and little if any heckling of our players. For once, Yankee Stadium didn't pack much punch.

GAME 6:
LEMON-AID

Strangely, such a tense World Series ended in a 9-2 blowout win for us. But the game might have been closer if not for a strategic maneuver by the Yankees manager that was second-guessed from the moment he made it. The pitching matchup was Hooton versus John, a rematch of the Game 2 duel that was won by John. Randolph put New York on the scoreboard first with a third-inning solo home run, but we tied it with a run in the fourth when Yeager singled home Baker from second with two out.

With the game still tied 1-1 and no designated hitter in the lineup, Lemon pinch-hit for John with two out and runners on first and second in the bottom of the fourth inning. As Murcer was preparing to walk to home plate to pinch-hit, John was pacing in the Yankees' first-base dugout, staring at Lemon and shaking his head in disbelief. Murcer flied out to the right field warning track—where I randomcatch the ball—to end the inning. He hit the ball hard—but not hard enough. On my way to our dugout, I saw John just standing there staring at his manager. The Stadium was silent, but our dugout was electric!

Yankees manager Bob Lemon—one of the nicest people in baseball—was placed on the firing line after the game to answer questions from the media. Bob didn't bat an eye in saying: "Burt Hooton was pitching good for them. I was trying to get some runs and then go to Goose Gossage in the seventh inning. I didn't know if we would get on base again. I used Murcer because I wanted a base hit, and he's my best contact hitter."

Lemon turned the game over to George Frazier, who was about to set a World Series record with his third loss. Asked later why he went with Frazier, Lemon said he thought the pitcher's luck would change. I know ours did. We scored three runs in the top of the fifth inning, capped by Guerrero's triple, which knocked in two runs. Then we blew it open with four more runs in the sixth, two of which were unearned due to an error by Nettles, of all people. Lopes and Russell successfully completed a double-steal in the inning, and Guerrero singled home two runs. In the eighth, Guerrero put an exclamation point on his breakthrough series performance with a solo homer, giving him five RBI in the game.

Howe, doing the unthinkable for a closer by today's definition, pitched the final 3⅔ innings in relief of Hooton, allowing just two hits and no runs. When Bob Watson's fly ball landed in Ken Landreaux's glove to end the game, we sealed the fifth World Series in Dodgers history. For me, it was a first.

10

PARTY TIME

A fter Ken Landreaux's glove snapped over the ball for the final out and Steve Howe leaped off the mound into a bear hug from my roomie, Steve Yeager, the party was on! We have all watched the victory celebrations on the field after a team wins a championship, but to finally experience that dramatic moment myself was out of this world!

Steve Garvey, however, was nearly knocked out of this world.

"I remember that fly ball, and as Ken Landreaux was waiting for it, I was drifting toward the mound for the obligatory mob scene," Garvey says. "And *Sports Illustrated* had a great photo of Steve Howe jumping about eight feet in the air and Steve Yeager putting a big hug on him. What most people didn't notice is that just as I got to the mound, Yeager spun Howe, and his elbow clocked me right on the chin. He caught me just right. My hat flew off and it dazed me for a second. That was the day I learned that I could take a punch. I was nearly knocked out cold. This was the highlight of my career, and I was practically knocked out on the mound."

The on-field victory celebration ended quickly after that, with no further KOs. There was some hugging and hollering, enough high-fives to last a lifetime, but we were still in what was known as "enemy territory." I quickly felt a sense of urgency to leave the field. It was a crazy feeling, and one that to this day I am not sure was shared by any of my teammates. Selfishly, this was *our* victory celebration, and I felt like the Yankee fans we had been forced to listen to for three World Series shouldn't be a part it. I couldn't wait to get to our locker room.

It only took a few minutes for us to leave the field and sprint up the short tunnel, make a turn, and reach the insanity of our locker room. The players' lockers had been covered with plastic to help protect their clothes and equipment. The room was already jammed with celebrating Dodger players and coaches, trainers and staff, most holding, drinking, spraying, or pouring champagne on each other. An odd fragrance filled up the room: a mixture of champagne, uniform sweat, and the added steam that found its way from the showers into the locker room.

People began to pour into the room after the team celebrated privately for a few minutes. In came the TV and newspaper reporters, cameramen, baseball officials, and other members of the Dodgers organization. If you were opposed to being drenched with champagne, this was not the place to hang out. It was wet, wild, and extremely loud. Since the weather was cold outside, most of the folks who entered the room were dressed appropriately for the occasion by wearing overcoats. I just hoped they were waterproof!

If you didn't have tears in your eyes yet, you would as soon as you felt the wonderful sting of world championship champagne. For the players, the emotions just flood the brain. The aches and pains endured throughout the year suddenly vanish, time seems to stop, and you're overwhelmed by a sense of pride and happiness.

Rookie Steve Sax gets the champagne shampoo from Joe Beckwith and Bobby Castillo after we beat the Yankees.

IT GETS EMOTIONAL

I thought I was holding up pretty well emotionally, but I was flooded by thoughts of people who helped me along the way to become a Major League Baseball player and a good person. From my Pony League coach, Joe Misbrenner, who was the first one to tell me I had the ability to play professional baseball if I worked hard enough; to my high school coach, Rueben Navarro, who gave me the confidence to reach out and hold onto my dreams; to Coach Bobby Winkles at Arizona State University, who taught me about having a passion for what you do and the importance of having integrity as you do it.

And of course I thought of my mother, who I knew was watching the celebration on television. I hoped she was celebrating, too. Regardless of how difficult things may have been for her for all those years holding our home together, she always made the time to encourage me to hold onto my dreams of playing baseball and to believe that—no matter how bleak things may seem at the moment—they can improve if you believe in yourself and put forth the effort. My hope would be that everyone could have as loving a mom as I was privileged to have.

That's when it all really hit me! As a kid who idolized Major League Baseball players and was lucky enough to grow up with a supporting cast of people who cared about me, to have been blessed with the ability to play baseball, to have been part of a College World Series Championship team and an All-America selection, to have been a Major League All-Star in both leagues, blessed with two beautiful children, and now this—a world championship? I lost it, right then and there. The tears were not caused by the champagne; they were the result of plain old human emotions.

I have been blessed in so many ways, this truly was a time to celebrate! When baseball commissioner Bowie Kuhn presented the World Championship Trophy to owner Peter O'Malley and general manager Al Campanis, on behalf of the entire Dodger organization, the feeling of pride and accomplishment was incredible.

ANOTHER VIEW

It was interesting to hear what the thrill of this victory meant to our younger teammates who lacked the perspective of having to previously experience the agony of defeat on this stage.

"Here it is, my first full year in the Major Leagues, and we've just won the World Series," recalls Mike Scioscia. "I looked around the clubhouse and saw Davey Lopes crying. I saw Dusty Baker and Reggie Smith and guys who strove their entire careers never knowing, but always hoping, that they'd be right there in that situation.

"I'm there thinking, 'This is cool, let's do it every year.' But I saw them and realized what an accomplishment it was and how difficult it was to win a World Series. And not just winning a World Series, but doing it at Yankee Stadium. That doesn't happen very often. It was just a magical year."

ORDER MORE HARDWARE

Ron Cey, Pedro Guerrero, and Yeager were called to a makeshift platform to announce that they had been named the World Series tri-MVPs. Game 6 of the World Series turned out to be the coming-out party for Guerrero, who would never again be a part-time player after this five-RBI show. Pete ended the series with a .333 average and two homers. Cey, meanwhile, hit .350 with one home run and six RBI, and of course returned from the broken arm near the end of the regular season and the beaning in Game 5. Yeager hit two home runs and a double, and drove in four runs—two of them game-winners. The trio shared the trophy, but you could have added a few more names to the MVP list. It was that kind of team effort that was needed for the Dodgers to win their first world championship since 1965.

Eventually the supply of champagne ran out. Empty bottles were everywhere. Beer was the next choice of liquid to add to the now overly saturated carpeting and steamy room. Tommy Lasorda had disappeared to the press interview room for a few minutes of questions from the members of the media—the sane ones—who had decided to stay dry and not enter the locker room. When Tommy finally returned, the celebrating started all over again as he preached about the "fruits of victory," yelling out "how sweet it is." Well, we didn't have any fruit, the champagne was all gone, the beer was running low,

Jerry Reuss (left), who pitched a complete game win in Game 5 of the World Series, takes time out of the food-fight celebration to pose with teammate Reggie Smith (right) after we won the world championship.

but we found some mayonnaise and mustard ... and Tommy got slathered with enough of that stuff to make the staff cry at the Carnegie Deli in New York City.

The celebration was wonderfully childish for a room full of grown men. Jerry Reuss, Terry Forster, Tom Niedenfuer, and Scioscia started a food fight. And there was a great one-liner from Jay Johnstone, who said that Reuss had the appearance of an abstract painting. Or, as Jay would also say, Jerry looked like Bill Russell after nine innings of trying to field those ground balls. Boys will be boys!

When things finally calmed down from the frenetic pitch that had occupied the locker room, and we finally got showered, the next goal was to hopefully find dry clothes still hanging in our individual lockers. The clubhouse guys, as it turned out, had done a marvelous job in covering our clothes, and most were still dry. However, with the champagne- and beer-drenched carpeting, the hardest part was trying to find even a tiny spot to stand to keep your socks and slacks dry when getting dressed.

How delightful it was to finally leave Yankee Stadium and New York City without hearing, yet again, "The Yankees are No. 1." *Finally!*

"You know," says Lasorda, "after we lost to the Yankees in 1977 and 1978, the only thing I wanted was to be able to get back to the World Series and beat them. I used to pray, 'Dear God, if you can see it in your heart, put me in another Fall Classic, please, because I want to beat the Yankees so bad.' And that's what happened, and we finally were rewarded for all of that hard work."

It was, Garvey thinks, the culmination of an era of Dodger baseball.

"Winning the championship did bring closure or symmetry to what was started. You can go all the way back to the '68 draft when most of us came together, to June 21, 1973, when the four components of the infield came together," Garvey says. "We played together for pretty much a decade, a most remarkable decade. And it culminated in a world championship, turning years of frustration into joy. The season started with Fernando Valenzuela carrying us, but it ended with a total team effort—a team destined to win."

A SORE BOSS

After the series, Yankees owner George Steinbrenner epitomized the words "sore loser." He apologized to the people of New York for his team's play. That ticked me off then and it ticked me off again when I read it recently in a book:

"I want to sincerely apologize to the people of New York and to the fans of the New York Yankees everywhere for the performance of the Yankee team in the World Series," he said. "I also want to assure you that we will be at work immediately to prepare for 1982. I want also to extend my congratulations to Peter O'Malley and the Dodger organization—a fine team that didn't give up—and to my friend, Tom Lasorda, who managed a superb season, playoff, and a brilliant World Series."

I actually felt sad for the Yankee team, which had just been slapped across the face publicly by their principal owner. They had nothing to apologize for. Dodger owner Peter O'Malley would never call out his players like that publicly. As team official Robert Schweppe recalled, the O'Malley way was "to be graceful in victory and humble in defeat."

"My initial reaction to that was, 'Hey, man, just admit that we beat you,'" Baker says. "I mean, you can't beat us all the time. That's the first thing I thought about. I mean the championship at that time doesn't necessarily have New York's name on it, you know?"

THE RING'S THE THING

Of all the symbols of success in sports, nothing carries the weight of a championship ring, which I finally won. Baker told me that sometimes he brings that World Series ring out when he manages because there's something magical about it.

"Sometimes I bring it out if we're in a losing streak now," says Baker. "That's the only time I wear it now, when I want to feel like a champion. It's like my She-Ra ring—I hold it up to the sky and I get some power. I do, sometimes.

"There are times when the only thing that keeps you going in bad times is trying to recall and remember how you felt as a champion during the good times. And most of it's psychological. When I look back on the guys on that team and how they busted it and how we believed it, you know, when no one else believed, there is something magical about it. It's no joke. That was one of the greatest years I ever spent in baseball."

Unless you're a player who's won a ring, or a player who never was able to, you really can't appreciate what "The Ring" really means.

"It means that I have something on my finger that so many men would love to have, that every little boy's dream is to have," says Yeager. "Every professional man I've ever come in contact with would like to trade places with me. I'm talking about doctors and lawyers and high executive people, even some judges. They've told me that for one day they'd like to go to the ballpark, put the uniform on, play the game, go out with us after the game, go to bed, and wake up the next morning and go back to their [real] work. They'd like to do it one time.

"I feel that I've got something on my finger that a lot of great players—one comes to mind, Ernie Banks—don't have. He's a Hall of Famer, Mr. Cub, and he doesn't have one. I've got something that he probably should've had in his career, but he doesn't have. ... I feel very fortunate and very lucky, that it's a symbol of achievement—reaching that goal, that dream that you had as a child and actually having an opportunity to fulfill it.

"Every day I wear it. I'm around these kids right now in Double-A, and they see this ring, and I say, 'It's not going to come easy. You've got to work for it; you've got to sacrifice for it; you've got to do the little things that it takes; you've got to learn how to play the game;

you've got to learn how to play together; you've got to learn how to have fun.'

"A lot of guys have gotten into the World Series several times and have never gotten a ring. I've got mine and it's an inspiration."

As for me, I wear my ring almost all the time. When we earned it in 1981, it brought everything full circle for the players, the coaching staff, and the front office of that team. By God, we did it!

11

NEVER GIVE UP

What a turnaround for the 1981 club. Three weeks before clinching the World Series title, we came limping back to Dodger Stadium having lost the first two games of the Western Division Playoffs to the Houston Astros. Some fans and reporters criticized manager Tommy Lasorda for waiting for home runs rather than trying to scratch out a run here and there. I had commented in the press at the time that we returned home needing three straight victories, and we were greeted by a "Missouri crowd. You know, Missouri—the 'show-me state.'" Well, we showed 'em, and our fans responded with an astonishing amount of vocal support.

We had to win two straight in Montreal to advance—and we did. And finally, we went down two games to none against the Yankees in the World Series before turning things around and accomplishing what many people thought was impossible. We championed a common declaration to perseverance: "Nothing is impossible if you never give up."

"I've got to be honest: I don't remember a damn thing about the plane ride back from New York," recalls Jerry Reuss. "But I do remember the celebration in the locker room, and to this day I remember the moment that they handed the World Championship Trophy to Al Campanis, our general manager, and Tommy Lasorda. And I remember to this day the pride that I felt for all of us in that room, because we fought against some terrific odds to even get there, much less to do it.

"I do remember the TV interviews with Tommy and Al and also Peter O'Malley. The Brooklyn Dodgers were Peter's father's team, and they faced off against the Yankees a number of times, finally winning a championship in 1955. Fast-forwarding again, to the Dodgers in Los Angeles in '77 and '78, Peter was more of an integral part of the front office at that time. In 1981, it was his club, because in '79, his father passed away. … This was Peter's time. And Peter, as well as Al and Tommy, each of them walked up there with, for lack of a better word, their own personal baggage, in a sense. For Peter, this was his first [solo] shot at a World Series, and he came out a winner, especially against the Yankees. So for him, the lifelong nemesis had been wiped out.

"Al had been a lifer in the Dodger organization, and so remembered what it was like—the heartbreak of losing to the Yankees all those years. He had some 40 or 50 years of ghosts following him around that were exorcised on that night.

"And as far as Tommy was concerned, it validated him as a manager. It was one thing to get to the World Series in your first full year as a Major League manager. And to get there the first two years that you manage, that's something, too. Making it there was a huge stepping-stone for him toward eventually going into the Hall of Fame. But I think for Tommy, he was still empty, because he didn't win. He got there, but he didn't win.

Club president Peter O'Malley (left) puts his arm around general manager Al Campanis, who constructed the roster that turned into the 1981 world champions.

"And then to go through what he did in '79 and '80. In '79 we were lousy, but in '80 we were so close, that when we finally got there in '81, it wiped away a number of disappointments for him that went back to the time he was a player.

"So you could see that they each had different stories as they stepped up on that podium and were presented with the World Championship Trophy. All that time, all that effort, all that heartache, and all those good times finally came to that point where all three of them could share it."

Jaime Jarrin, the club's longtime Spanish-language broadcaster, called the season the most spectacular he'd ever seen.

"From Fernando's first pitch to Guerrero's home run in the final World Series game, it was a season full of surprises and excitement and drama as we've never seen before," he says. "Even 1963 (when the Dodgers swept the Yankees) wasn't as dramatic. This was the most exciting season in Los Angeles Dodger history."

A CITY REJOICES

To say the trip back to Los Angeles that night was enjoyable is like saying that a 10-year-old "kind of likes" opening his presents on Christmas morning. The passengers on that airplane were happy and proud 10-year-olds who just happened to be grown men. Captain Lew Carlisle could have done aileron rolls and loops all the way back to California, and I doubt if we would have noticed.

We landed at LAX airport with the happiest group of fans waiting all over the airport to welcome us back home. One gentleman even walked with me all the way to my car, recalling almost every play of Game 6 each step of the way.

"I don't think that anybody in any place could have a better support system than what we had," says Ron Cey. "And we became family. There were times when our fans could've booed us, but they almost took us as family, as being their kids. It's as if they were saying, 'Don't spank him, don't go in there and yell at him, but let him have his bad week or whatever he's going to have, because everything's going to be fine.'

"They just let us get through our tough times with the least amount of flak, and we gave them all the entertainment in the world. Four World Series in eight years, and essentially an all-All-Star infield. I think every member of our '81 regular eight was an All-Star at some point in time. That kind of stuff really doesn't happen very often. And what we got in return was their support. We gave them the entertainment, years they will never forget—and we won't either."

When I got home and closed the front door, all of the sounds from the last three weeks were finally cut off. After so much drama and excitement over that period of time, the sudden sound of silence was deafening.

I couldn't wait to find the newspaper the next morning. The *L.A. Times* featured a visual feast of images that I will remember for a lifetime. Pictures of people who became teammates, who became friends, and who ultimately became part of Major League Baseball history. A snippet in time that will forever be documented when our team, the 1981 Los Angeles Dodgers, became the world champions!

The team had a parade through the streets of downtown Los Angeles and received congratulations from dignitaries around the world. President Ronald Reagan wrote: "All the world loves a winner, but, most of all, we love a winner who has a heart. Your courage and determination in overcoming early setbacks are baseball at its inspiring best. I'm sure the 'Great Dodger in the Sky' is pleased."

We had a party at Dodger Stadium after the parade. I remember a great article about the team in *Sports Illustrated* written by Ron Fimrite that captured what the championship meant to the members of the '81 team. As Fimrite chronicled, the wine was flowing freely, there were a lot of flowers, there was a band that was playing, but there was an underlying feeling that while we were rejoicing at finally winning the World Series, some of us were going to be gone very soon. As Fimrite wrote: "Eat, drink and be merry, for tomorrow you could be traded to San Diego."

He pretty much nailed the mood. I really felt that the celebration was rather hollow, because we really did not know who was going to be around come spring training in 1982.

"We could've probably stayed together another two or three years," says Cey. "But that probably would have ruined the Dodgers' way of doing things, and wouldn't have allowed some of their younger players—like they did with us—to come in and get some things started. This new group of guys eventually turned out to be a lot like us. The only difference is that [when we came up] we weren't replacing guys like us, guys who went to four World Series, were All-Stars, and had etched themselves in the Dodger record books. We were replacing guys who should've been replaced, who hadn't done much. So there was a lot of pressure on the young guys, I think, to achieve."

BEGINNING OF THE END

The 1981 title was the culmination of a decade of frustration. But it also hastened the roster's dismantling, which management began immediately. First to go was Davey Lopes, traded in the offseason to Oakland for a Minor Leaguer. Reggie Smith was granted free agency and signed with the Giants. Pitchers Rick Sutcliffe and Bobby Castillo were also dealt in the offseason. Following the 1982 season, Garvey and Terry Forster became free agents and signed with the Padres and the Braves, and Cey was traded to the Cubs.

"Davey left, and Garvey left and Cey left—all within a year—and that kind of destroyed the [family] feeling," says Steve Yeager. "Once you play the game long enough and stay together long enough, you know that somebody's going to come along and replace you—it's just a matter of time.

"But to me the timing wasn't right, because, hell, we'd just won, and we weren't very old. You know, we were still capable of probably putting together another two or three good seasons. Who knows … we could've maybe made it back to the World Series with the ball club that we had, if they'd held it together."

It's true. I re-signed with the Dodgers less than a month after being granted free agency after the 1981 season ended. And I stuck around until 1984, when my career ended after 19 long seasons. We can wonder, "What if that club had remained together another couple seasons? Could we have won another?" But at least we can say for certain: We finally won one!

ACKNOWLEDGMENTS

T his project was made possible through the extraordinary efforts of our editor at Sports Publishing, Doug Hoepker. We also were greatly assisted by the Amateur Athletic Foundation Library, Dusty Baker, Steve Brener, Ron Cey, Steve Garvey, Colin Gunderson, Jim Hill, Jaime Jarrin, Mark Langill, Tommy Lasorda, Frank McCourt, Jamie McCourt, Peter O'Malley, Josh Rawitch, Jerry Reuss, Bill Russell, Robert Schweppe, Mike Scioscia, Vin Scully, Mark Thoma, Steve Yeager, and Toby Zwikel.

Finally, this book is dedicated to my patient and loving wife, Sheryl; my adorable daughter, Kelsey; the world's strongest woman, my Mom; and in memory of Dad, my hero.

–Ken Gurnick

Celebrate the Heroes of Baseball

in These Other New and Recent Releases from Sports Publishing!